HEARER OF THE WORD

HEARER OF THE WORD

Laying the Foundation for a Philosophy of Religion

KARL RAHNER

Translation of the First Edition by
Joseph Donceel

Edited and with an Introduction by
Andrew Tallon

Continuum • New York

1994

The Continuum Publishing Company
370 Lexington Avenue
New York, NY 10017

First edition of *Hörer des Wortes.*
Zur Grundlegung einer Religionsphilosophie
published by ©Verlag Kösel-Pustet, Munich, 1941

Translation from the First Edition by Joseph Donceel, S.J.
English translation copyright ©1994 by Joseph Donceel, S.J.

Library of Congress Cataloguing-in-Publication Data

Rahner, Karl, 1904-84
    [Hörer des Wortes. English]
    Hearer of the Word. Laying the Foundation for a
        Philosophy of Religion: translated by Joseph Donceel.
    Includes bibliographical references.
    ISBN 0-8264-0648-3 (alk. paper)
    1. Religion–Philosophy. 2. Knowledge, Theory of (Religion)
I. Title.
BL51.R2413   1994
180–dc20   93-38427
                                                                  CIP

Printed in the United States of America

HEARER OF THE WORD

Table of Contents

Translator's Preface

The German edition of this book, which bears the title *Hörer des Wortes*, was published by Kösel-Pustet in München in 1941. It followed closely upon Karl Rahner's other important book on philosophy, *Geist in Welt*, which was published in 1939 by Rauch in Innsbruck.

When these two works come out Karl Rahner was a young unknown Jesuit. *Geist in Welt* was his Ph.D. dissertation, with which he had run into serious difficulties at the University of Freiburg. His mentor, Professor Martin Honecker, disapproved so strongly of the way in which his pupil interpreted the philosophy of Thomas Aquinas that he rejected the dissertation. Honecker read Aquinas the way he was then being read by most neo-Thomists. But Rahner had been deeply influenced by the Aquinas interpretation of his Belgian fellow Jesuit, Joseph Maréchal, through whose monumental work, *Le Point de Départ de la Métaphysique*, he had valiantly worked his way. In his dissertation he took over Maréchal's main ideas, especially the conviction that, because of the dynamism of our human intellect, we implicitly affirm the existence of God in every judgment and free activity. This bold conception of our relation to the Absolute was to become the trademark of Rahner's philosophy and theology. Nor did he simply take over this idea. Right from the start, in *Geist in Welt*, it became evident that Rahner was not merely a disciple, but an original thinker. He worked out and deepened Maréchal's basic intuition; he rephrased it in a new terminology, which is partly borrowed from another of his Freiburg professors, Martin Heidegger. And in his *Hörer des Wortes* he applied it, with great skill and originality, to a study of the philosophy of religion, to a thorough investigation of the relation between philosophy and theology.

Hörer des Wortes grew out of a series of lectures delivered during a 1937 Summer School at Salzburg, Austria. As the author himself mentioned in the Preface of the first 1941 edition, this fact explains some of the peculiarities of the book:

> The fifteen chapters of this book are a transcription of fifteen lectures delivered quite a while ago at a theological Summer School. This origin explains their peculiar nature: they intend to provide in a few pages a general idea of a rather wide topic. They contain no bibliography. They have about the same length, regardless of the matter treated. They do not discuss diverging opinions. They contain a few references to my work *Geist in Welt. Zur Metaphysik der endlichen Erkenntnis bei Thomas von Aquin* (Innsbruck 1939). [*Hörer des Wortes*, p. 7. Arntsdorf, Christmas, 1940—Karl Rahner.]

Both important books came out at a most unpropitious time, the first two years of the Second World War. Although, as a result, they did not, especially outside of Germany, receive the attention they deserved, they keep selling, so that a reprinting became necessary. The author would have liked to rework them and bring them up to date. But he had meanwhile started on a prodigious career in theology, which was very soon to make of him one of the leading thinkers in the Catholic Church. There was no time for a revision of his earlier philosophical works.

He entrusted the task to one of his most brilliant pupils, who was eventually to become an original thinker in his own right, Johannes Baptist Metz. Metz brought out a slightly revised edition of *Geist in Welt* in 1957, which came out, five years later, in an excellent English translation: *Spirit in World*, translated by William Dych, S.J., New York, Herder & Herder, 1968.

In 1963 Metz published the revised edition of *Hörer des Wortes*. An English translation of this revised edition came out in 1969: *Hearers of the Word*, translated by Michael Richards, New York, Herder & Herder, 1969.

Metz has put much more of his own into this second revision. Quite understandably so. He wished to transform the work from a series of lectures into a regular book. In a series of lectures the lecturer summarizes his main ideas at the end of each talk, and, once more, at the beginning of the following talk. Metz eliminated these repetitions. Moreover he introduced into the text and into the voluminous notes added to the original work, a number of corrections and expansions, as well as references to his own writings and to the writings of Rahner.

Although Karl Rahner endorsed all the changes introduced by his colleague into his original work, although Metz magnanimously published the work under the sole name of the Master, it is difficult to escape the impression that we are no longer reading a genuine Rahner work. This would not matter much if Rahner had not meanwhile developed into the leading theologian of the Catholic Church. His works are slowly turning into classics. Many scholars wish to read him "straight" and are willing to overlook occasional repetitions and other minor flaws in order to get at his personal ideas.

The French translation of the book (K. Rahner–J.B. Metz, *L'Homme à l'écoute du Verbe*, traduction et édition comparée par J. Hofbeck. Paris, Mame, 1967) provides its readers with a translation both of Metz's revised edition and of Rahner's original work. For this purpose it uses different kinds of print and plenty of brackets and parentheses. The outcome is a book which is even more difficult to read than either of the German works, which are difficult enough in their own right.

That is why the American publisher, after bringing out in 1969 an English translation of Metz's revised edition, publishes hereby a translation of the original German text of 1941.

Classics never really age. The reader may find this out once more by studying this remarkable work on the foundations of the philosophy of religion.

Joseph Donceel, S.J.
Fordham University

Editor's Introduction
(Being Some Historical & Technical Notes)

A Little Background on this Text

Father Donceel wrote the above Preface many years ago thinking his translation was due out soon. In fact it never appeared in the way he had hoped. (There was a partial publication of it in Gerald McCool's *A Rahner Reader.*) We are now very much in his debt for this excellent translation of the first German edition (HW1), at last being officially published for the first time.

Some years ago (about 1969) Father Donceel sent me a carbon copy of his private translation (HW1E), still at that time in the process of being revised, so that I could avoid using the totally unacceptable Richards translation (of HW2) for my graduate students. With permission of Crossroad Publishing Co., I had HW1E retyped, incorporating all of Donceel's numerous handwritten corrections, and printed a limited edition of 100 copies. Donceel also graciously allowed certain others to use his translation and it lived a useful life circulating in this way for over two decades. Colleagues and students found typos, suggested revisions, etc., and many hands contributed in one way or another to this translation. Thomas Sheehan, of Loyola University (Chicago), was the most helpful of all.

It has also circulated for almost ten years in disk form. When I founded *Philosophy & Theology* in 1986, permission was kindly extended by Crossroad to publish a computer disk edition of HW1E as one of the disk supplements to the journal (which appears in both hardcopy and disk subscription forms). Part of the history of this text includes the fact that several years ago the Karl Rahner Society of America adopted *Philosophy & Theology* as its official journal; the Autumn issue each year is devoted to Rahner and his philosophy and theology. A feature of that issue is the Annual Update of the Bibliography of Rahner as Subject;

the complete bibliography is available as a separate disk and is a useful research tool for scholars. I mention these things because it will be of great interest to Rahner scholars to know that Continuum, the new publisher of both *Spirit in the World*—simultaneously being newly published in a thoroughly corrected version—and *Hearer of the Word*, have kindly granted permission to Marquette University Press to publish disk versions of both of these new editions of Rahner's two philosophical classics. They will be valuable research instruments for all scholars and students of Rahner.

It was only relatively recently that the Metz/Richards version of HW2 went out of print (*Deo gratias*). In December 1993, Mr. Frank Oveis, Director of the newly formed separate Continuum Publishing Co., decided to publish the Joseph Donceel translation. Here was cause for the world of Rahner scholarship to celebrate! My task, in addition to a thorough editing, was to write a brief Introduction explaining the technical side of this retrieval of the original edition. I had published a very detailed analysis of HW2E in *The Thomist* in 1974,[1] comparing the two German editions, noting the Hofbeck French translation (HWF), and strongly criticizing the Richards translation. I was certainly not alone in being dissatisfied: all attempts by Rahner and Donceel to have HW2E withdrawn were futile. Metz had made over 1300 changes to Rahner's text; readers of HW2 and HW2E never knew whether they were reading Rahner or Metz. Also, HW1 had only one note of its own; all the other many notes in HW2 (123 of them) were Metz's. Finally, since Metz eventually became a major critic of Rahner, it became important for Rahner scholars to have access to his own text.

Things Revised, in General

As we all unthinkingly did, not so long ago, Father Donceel used "man" for *Mensch*, the generic man-and-woman, male-female. So one editorial task has been to achieve gender neutral or inclusive language, by substituting "human being," "human nature," or some other term for the German "*Mensch*," etc., by using "humanity" or "humankind" for *Menschheit*, and by using "we" and "our" instead of alternating between the cumbersome "he, she, his, her," etc., in appropriate situations. "Human being" fit best where the context showed comparison with "being," e.g., a "being" (*Seiende*) and "being" (*Sein*). Where Donceel had often added "the act of" before *Sein*, I have instead let the context show clearly the contrast between "being" and [a] "being" (*Sein und Seiende*), not choosing to capitalize "Being" in order to avoid suggesting divinity where it is inappropriate; Rahner says God where he means God. Rahner also sometimes used *Person* (and *Persönlichkeit*) himself, leading me to prefer "person" and "human person" in some contexts. Numbers in brackets refer to the German edition.

Some Particular Terms

Some important words and their translations may now be discussed; again, please refer to the articles mentioned in note 1 for earlier and, in some cases, more detailed treatment. The following observations may be considered complementary to those, except in the cases of *Nachvollzug, Geworfenheit, Bewegung*, and *Vorgriff*.

Inner Moment: *inner* (the German word) usually (not always) is better translated "intrinsic" than "inner" since not space (or physical contiguity or coherence) or interiority but connection or logical or essential cohesion is meant. *Moment* is a *faux ami*, a pseudo-cognate that has nothing to do with time (as in "a moment in time") but is connected with motion (as in "momentum"), importance (as in something "of moment," a "momentous" occasion), and constitution (and here the best translation is usually "element," "component," "constituent," sometimes including necessity).

Geworfenheit: Metz suppressed this Heideggerian word, substituting *Zufälligkeit* ("contingency" or "fortuitousness"). But since Rahner himself used both *Geworfenheit* ("thrownness"; *geworfen*, "thrown") and *Zufälligkeit*, I have restored "thrownness" and "thrown," not to call attention to Heidegger's influence — that need not be done since it is Rahner himself who calls the word Heidegger's — but to distinguish "thrown" and "thrownness" from "contingent" and "contingency." Rahner clearly takes "thrown" to mean "contingent," and uses the two words in apposition on one occasion. He does, however, sometimes use "thrown" and sometimes "contingent," so the translation respects his usages.

Bewegung, Zielbewegung. The German words have occasionally been supplied in brackets in order to highlight the important idea of movement, motion, *kinesis*, temporality, etc., associ-
ated with Rahner's Heidegger-inspired idea of human finiteness
in its relation to the horizon of being. Rahner discusses his interpretation of the term, goal, end, *telos*, finality of human action as
that contrasts with Heidegger's, and interested readers should
consult Thomas Sheehan's penetrating discussion in his excellent and highly recommended study *Karl Rahner.*[2]

*Nachvollzug, nachvollziehen, sich vollziehen, Vollzug, mitvollziehen,
Mitvollzug.* These words, favorites of Rahner (and Emerich
Coreth), suggest a drawing (*ziehen*; cf. German *Zug*, train) to a
full (*voll*) or complete actualization, although the *voll* or "full"
aspect is not always emphasized. I have previously[3] recommended
"to enact" for *vollziehen*, with "enacting" or "enactment" for *Vollzug*,
"self-enacting" or "self-enactment" for *Selbstvollzug*, depending
on contexts. I have heard from colleagues who have found this
term helpful. *Vollzug* has elsewhere been translated as "exercise,"
"operation," "consummation" and other words found in German
dictionaries. Lonergan preferred "performance"[4] because it allowed him to contrast an act or operation of intelligent consciousness (e.g., an insight) with its expression (e.g., a concept); the
self-enacting and self-appropriating subject is the ultimate crite-
rion of being, not what appears to sense intuition (the *conversio
ad phantasma*, in Thomist language) limited to space and time.
As Lonergan would say, consciousness (like being) is analogous
to the level on which it is experienced, whether that be the first
or the fourth (or even fifth, in Lonergan's structural schema),
and Rahner and Lonergan concur in finding the human spirit
defined not by the limits of temporality and sense intuition but
by the dynamism of intentional consciousness (*Vorgriff*) as we
move through these levels, from experience, through understanding, into critical judgment, and on finally to responsible decision
and action, all against the background of affective consciousness experienced as feelings and the immediate attitudes and
dispositions we call moods. They would also concur in allowing
for a fifth level of consciousness, where the action of the spirit
(analogous to human love), bestowing the gifts (which are vir-

tues, i.e., habits like faith, love, and hope) that can transform consciousness "from the top down," as it were, can be interpreted as bringing about a new recognition that the limit of consciousness may not even be set by human intentionality at all but by the free initiative of a God who chooses to speak a word in history and, in the process, empower (the obediential potency) us to hear it.

Now *Nachvollzug* shares in the many options based on the root *vollziehen*. Adding *nach* can mean (1) "in direction toward" (*nach Berlin*), (2) "after," as temporal, later than (*nach Christi*), (3) "after," as spatial, behind (*nach mir*), and/or (4) "according to" or "in relation to" (*nach meiner Ansicht/Meinung*). "Following in someone's footsteps" touches on this idea of modeling one's life or values on a paradigm, integrating another's choices into one's own, making another's decisions one's own, by a kind of identification in practice and performance; thus it is a co-enactment, a co-performance. *Mitvollziehen* suggests co-enactment but with perhaps too much simultaneity, while *Nachvollziehen* acknowledges another's leadership or initiative, such as God's freely speaking the word when we could not claim it as our due or demand it as necessary fulfilment of our nature.

Again, with Lonergan's help, we could say that mediated self-appropriation is suggested. *Nachvollzug* would be a self-appropriation of some truth or value through the mediation of that truth or value by someone else, e.g., someone who embodies such truth or value. Mediated immediacy, the chief function of language, and *Nachvollzug* would therefore seem to have much in common, a self-actualization that could not happen without the help of the other; in this context, it would mean making one's own the word spoken in history to humankind centuries ago and ever echoing today. Sheehan (in his *Karl Rahner*, p. 179) suggests "retrieval" for *Nachvollzug*, recalling the Heideggerian inspiration. "Ratification," Donceel's single word for *Nachvollzug*, does contain the gist of the idea, but, without added clarification (such as the above hints), it seems to me, it could leave the reader with the false impression that a far less personal and demanding gesture is being implied, a mere mental assent rather than a total commitment of the whole person in full, triune consciousness, including one's affection, cognition, and volition, both heart and head.

Vorgriff. Let us finally come to the famous and much discussed *Vorgriff.* Here, as with other key terms, a misleading translation can end up leading to a misapprehension.[5] *Vorgriff* means "anticipation" in ordinary German. "Anticipation"[6] is the safest translation and Donceel occasionally simply used that word, especially in the gerund or participle form, and usually translating *vorgreifend*; I have usually placed the German in brackets to alert the reader. In the context of metaphysics of cognition (*Erkenntnismetaphysik*), however, we find it used as a *terminus technicus* and Donceel chose not to translate it and it has seemed best to me to follow his practice (he also chose not to translate *Nachvollzug* sometimes, but I have not followed that practice). Not translating *Vorgriff* is the reason for the definite article "the," usually found with *Vorgriff.*

What have to be avoided are translations that even hint that there is something like an apprehension (presumably an impossible grasping of the horizon—being [*Sein*]—before the apprehension of the object—a being [*Seiende*]—grasped on this side of the horizon). Thus "pre-apprehension," or, worse, "pre-concept" (see the Richards translation of HW2), neither of which is Donceel usage, need to be avoided or used with caution: *vorgreifen* is not *vorbegreifen*; *Vorgriff* is not *Vorbegriff.* Rahner himself is very explicit that the act named *Vorgriff* is not even necessarily cognitive, but makes cognition possible (along with the other two modes of consciousness, affection and volition). Beyond what I said years ago, about the "reaching out toward without grasping," let me add only the following.

If we overcome some of our resistance to tampering with Rahner's word, as though out of reverence for it, we might, without prejudice, suggest that in fact it means essentially (though not exactly) the same thing that others have called *excessus* (Aquinas), intentionality (Husserl), transcendence (Heidegger), existence (Merleau-Ponty), even responsibility (Levinas), admittedly without claiming perfect identification among these concepts, as though that were ever possible in philosophy. If we contrast the "pure" or "idealistic" intentionality of Husserl, where intentions terminate intramentally at representations in consciousness, with the "existential" phenomenology of Heidegger and most of the German and French philosophers who follow him, where intentionality as consciousness (and emphatically as embodiment, in Levinas and Merleau-Ponty), characterizes human being in-the-world (*in-ðer-Welt*; innerworldly, *innerweltlich*), we have enough to make a beginning in the direction of retrieving the core of Rahner's philosophy of religion: something/someone *in* the world speaks for something/someone *beyond* the world, where world, as the space-time continuum of sense intuition, is known *as* a world only when it is implicitly (at first) and explicitly (in philosophy) objectified in the movement (*kinesis, Bewegung, Zielbewegung*) of consciousness transcending the world toward we know not where (*worauf*: whither), toward being as horizon of triune consciousness.

Calling the horizon of the *Vorgriff* "being" escapes not naming it "X," i.e., an unknown quantity to be solved for as any other heuristic structure, and this name is justified because in actual judgments we use the language of being for the finite objects that we do in fact affirm. It is not that we first know "being," as though as an object and in a concept (or pre-concept) and then name the objects after the horizon, but vice versa: we name the horizon after the beings. This occurs at Lonergan's third level of consciousness, where *being* is predicated, not at the second, where *essence* is conceptualized as a result of insight. Beyond "God's being," a negative theology tries to say something positive about "God's essence" by affirming the content of our concepts reached at the second level of cognitive consciousness and then denying their limits in order to affirm of "God" those qualities in the superlative. Everyone knows this to be a speculative venture at best, although in a very conservative form, i.e., based on and limited to the isomorphism between essence and being and the overall *structure* of consciousness, on the one hand, rather than based on its *content*, on the other, the method can serve the purpose Rahner's transcendental Thomism sets for it, viz., to show that revelation is possible; once that is established, it is up to each of us, as a potential hearer of the word, to listen for the word in history. All content must come from history.

Finite consciousness tries to overcome its finitude through embodying, emanating the affectability (*conversio*) that is its only intuition. Merleau-Ponty rethought Husserl's meaning of intentionality, emphatically investing embodiment with the "of-ness" Husserl found only in consciousness, characterizing the body (the person moving in space-time) thus:

The reason why I am able to understand the other person's body and existence 'beginning with' the body proper, the reason why the compresence of my 'consciousness' and my 'body' is prolonged into the compresence of my self and the other person, is that the 'I am able to' and the 'the other person exists' belong here and now to the same world, that the body proper is a premonition of the other person, the *Einfühlung* an echo of my incarnation, and that a flash of meaning makes them substitutable in the absolute presence of origins. Thus all of constitution is anticipated in the fulguration of *Urempfindung*.[7]

In other words, my body (i.e., embodiment as consciousness's first otherness) is a *Vorgriff*, a corporeal, connatural anticipation of another person. As emanation of spirit, sensibility makes consciousness present in space-time as affection (*Einfühlung, Urempfindung*), then as cognition and volition. Thus Rahner uses *Woraufhin* (whither, whereunto) both for spirit's (intellect's) anticipation of its horizon (being, truth) *and* for sensibility's anticipation of its horizon (beings in space-time). To demystify *Vorgriff* is to show its root meaning in intentionality *emphatically as embodied* and thus we get beyond a purely cognitive reading of *Vorgriff* and recognize in HW that *Vorgriff* opens the horizon of *all* being (whether or not we say [with Rousselot] that the human "I am able to" toward being stems from a deeper *capax Dei*, so that the "mystical" makes possible the "ethical" (the other person) and the historical (philosophy of religion, the anticipated advent of God in space-time). Levinas wrote in 1930 of affective intentionality as the necessary anticipation and completion of Husserl's representational intentionality. We need to recognize as a necessary continuation of HW an ethical apriori in the *Vorgriff*: the human composite is a premonition anticipating another person, the ethical human other; in my judgment, Rahner's anthropological turn means [with Levinas] that this ethical anticipation precedes and makes possible the revelation by the divine person in history.

Thus the *Vorgriff* is a nonrepresentational intentionality that makes possible all the actual operations of triune consciousness (affection, cognition, volition as inseparable but clearly distinguishable from one another). For this reason, Blondel's *l'action*, or rather the intrinsic dynamic structure of finite spirit revealed in action, with all its implications for consciousness, is perhaps the major inspiration behind Rahner's reading of Aquinas, mediated by Rousselot and Maréchal.[8] When one surveys the range of approaches to the human condition currently available in philosophy and theology, there is none that continues to have the unity, power, and attraction exercised by Rahner's. It is not difficult to account for it. It takes the best from a philosophy of spiritual dynamism that has never ceased to fascinate philosophers and theologians of a metaphysical leaning from the Greeks, Bonaventure, and Aquinas on; in modern times, Kant set his seemingly impossible agenda of transcending sense intuition while still recognizing that we can begin nowhere else and must always return there; and Hegel showed, in what he off-puttingly called "logic" (but what was really just another analysis of the immanent dynamic orientation of finite spirit to absolute spirit), that human consciousness itself, with its own structure, which he ultimately treated too statically, is the only arena of being. Blondel and Levinas followed Hegel from a distance by sublating him, one with a volitional intentionality, the other with an affective intentionality found to be actively operating prior to any volitional or cognitional intentionality. I believe I speak for many students of Rahner in saying that one of the most impressive things about his philosophy and theology is that its capacity for unlimited development lies in the openness of his metaphysical anthropology to the earlier influences that formed his thought (obviously Thomas Aquinas being the most significant) *and* to the later influences that improved it, both those within the Thomist tradition, and already in lively dialogue with contemporary thought (such as Rousselot and Maréchal) and those outside it. Rahner himself would be both complimented and complemented were his students to do as he himself did, as he showed the way, by trying in every imaginable, conceivable, and responsible way to continue and expand his dialogue with contemporary philosophy, theology, and science.

It is not with postmodern thought, at least in its currently dominant form, that the most promising dialogue has developed (or will develop) but with a "postmodernism" of a different sort, one we could call a "humanism of the other," or "ethics as first philosophy."

No one reading Blondel today can fail to mark the amazing similarity between his work and that of Emmanuel Levinas, whose primacy of the ethical over the ontological also places the dynamism of consciousness not in representations, not considering them the highest human actualization in a kind of rationalism or idealism, but in deeper dual affectivity; first, in a completely nonintentional affectivity, which can be interpreted as our preconscious created solidarity with all humanity as an apriori that transcends autonomous freedom in favor of prior responsibility for others; and second, in an affective intentionality when we encounter concrete others in face-to-face proximity, dethroning the ego and shocking us awake from our ethical slumber. It is not an exaggeration, therefore, to say that Levinas's "responsibility," based on this dual affectivity, a synthesis of nonrepresentational nonintentional affectivity and affective intentionality, is very close to the meaning of the *Vorgriff* as a movement becoming consciousness in all its inseparable triuneness but prior to distinctions into affection, cognition, and volition, a union of head and heart, the *appetitus naturalis* or *desiderium naturale* for transcendental otherness that for persons must ultimately be personal, as a finality connatural to us would demand. In this light, it is striking to compare the subtle debate about Blondel's method of immanence, and about the so-called errors of modernism, supposedly claiming too much of an exigency for God in our nature, with the opposite direction that popular postmodernism has taken.

Conclusion

"The greatest Catholic theologian of the twentieth century" — for nearly fifty years this is how we have been describing Karl Rahner. Today his reputation is more solid than ever: he has become the one to challenge, even to attack. Judging by the entries in the "Annual Bibliography of Rahner as Subject," interest in his work continues to grow. As we head into the third Christian millennium, there is every indication that a foundation in Rahner will be the ticket to theology's agenda for the twenty-first century.

The "paleo-Thomism" of Rahner's youthful instruction came alive only when he confronted it with the philosophical and religious crises of his young adult years, the years that became WW II. In his late twenties and early thirties he forged the basic method and positions of his metaphysical anthropology, presented in *Spirit in the World* and *Hearer of the Word* in a style that allows (indeed requires) the reader to think along with the master. Those foundations were the necessary tools he implicitly and sometimes explicitly used to address every major and many a minor theological question of our day. He found deep resources in a reading of Aquinas that would not have been possible had there not been Kant, Hegel, Blondel, Husserl, Rousselot, Maréchal, Heidegger.

Rahner taught us to be fearless in seeking truth from any human quarter, and his equally unrestricted devotion to teaching and preaching the truth meant he was often in trouble with Rome. Now, after a half century of intense scrutiny from all sides, his once radical thought seems the soul of orthodoxy. One can only conclude that most suspicion came from misunderstanding.

Rahner has been judged difficult of access by even his most ardent disciples, but often the reason is their having skipped his two essential philosophical works, without which no one should expect his theology to be clear. Ideally one should work diligently through both *Spirit in the World* and *Hearer of the Word*, the former first; but one should never, if forced to choose between them, forgo *Hearer of the Word*. In *Hearer of the Word* we have the single most accessible and necessary book of philosophy and pretheology Rahner ever wrote. It discusses not only being and knowledge, but freedom, faith, and love; it has a heart in a way missing from the necessarily technical tome that is *Spirit in the World*. It is the *sine qua non* of Rahner studies. A work of sustained power and incomparable metaphysical interest and importance, it is at once profound, yet readable and clear—at least in this excellent new translation of the first edition.

Hearer of the Word is a contemporary classic, the best key to understanding Rahner's *omnia opera*, and his single best effort to show how the human spirit in the world can hear the word of the Spirit who enters human history.

Andrew Tallon
Marquette University

Notes

1. "Spirit, Freedom, History. Karl Rahner's *Hörer des Wortes* (*Hearers of the Word*), *The Thomist* 33 (1974) 908-36. Two lines somehow failed to get printed (leaving footnote four with no anchor in the text), so I take this opportunity to restore them. Paragraph two should read:

> To interpret *Hörer des Wortes* it is helpful to note its setting. In 1939 Rahner completed his doctoral dissertation in philosophy. Two years before it was published as his first major work, *Geist in Welt*,[4] Rahner presented a series of fifteen lectures "on laying the foundation for a philosophy of religion." The primary aim of the dissertation had been to offer a metaphysics of human knowledge based on Thomas Aquinas. ...

A few years earlier I had published an article on SW2 entitled "Spirit, Matter, Becoming: Karl Rahner's *Spirit in the World* (*Geist in Welt*), *The Modern Schoolman*, 48 (1971) 151-65. Interested readers will find discussions, some of them extended, of key terms found in GW and HW; I will presume some acquaintance with those discussions, rather than repeat them, in order to keep this Introduction shorter. Some of the key terms discussed therein are: 1. *Beisichsein* and *Bei-dem-Andern-Sein*; 2. *Horizont*; *Medium, Moment*; 3. *Seinsmächtigkeit* (*Seinsmäßigkeit, Seinshabe*); 4. *Vollzug* and *Selbstvollzug*; 5. *Vorgriff*; 6. *Worauf, Woraufhin, Woran* (as nouns). Some of these terms were again discussed in the *Thomist* article on HW2E, but more briefly.

2. *Karl Rahner: The Philosophical Foundations* (Athens: Ohio University Press, 1987), especially in Chapter III, "Heidegger: A Rahnerian Reading," pp. 103-32, but also in the preceding chapter, "Rousselot and Maréchal: Transcendental Thomism," pp. 55-102, especially 67-73. A fully formed interpretation of the meaning of *Vorgriff* depends on deciding whether human *kinesis* is ultimately and exclusively temporal, i.e., with no possible still point beyond time, on the one hand, or admits of issue through faith in a God who is able to enter time and speak the word that allows the "access through excess" that is the *Vorgriff*, on the other, i.e., a noncognitive being-affected by God that is the gift of faith, one of the gifts of the spirit, virtues that transform consciousness without enlightening the mind in a conceptual way. More on this in the discussion of *Vorgriff*.

Editor's Introduction   xxi

See also my "The Heart in Rahner's Philosophy of Mysticism."
Theological Studies 53 (1992) 700-28. Other studies of mine relevant to
Rahner: *Personal Becoming. Karl Rahner's Metaphysical Anthropology.* Fore-
word by Karl Rahner, S.J. (Milwaukee: Marquette University Press,
1982). "The Meaning of the Heart Today: Revising a Paradigm with
Levinas and Rahner," *Journal of Religious Studies* 11(1984) 59-74. "Karl
Rahner—Philosopher (1904-1984)," *Philosophy Today* 28 (1984) 102-
04. "Connaturality in Aquinas and Rahner. A Contribution to the Heart
Tradition," *Philosophy Today* 28 (1984) 138-47. "Religious Belief and the
Emotional Life: Faith, Love, and Hope in the Heart Tradition," in *The
Life of Religion: Philosophy and the Nature of Religious Belief* (Washington
DC: University Press of America, 1986; ed. S. Harrison and R. Taylor)
17-38. "Affectivity in Ethics: Lonergan, Rahner, and Others in the Heart
Tradition," in *Religion and Economic Ethics,* ed. J. Gower (Lanham MD:
University Press of America, 1990) 87-122. "The Experience of God in
Relation to Rahner's Philosophy of the Heart," *Philosophy & Theology* 7
(1992) 193-210. "Prophecy, Prayer, and Affectivity: For a Religion of
the Heart," in *Louvain Philosophical Studies 6,* Vol. 2, ed. D.A. Boileau
and J.A. Dick (Leuven: Leuven University Press, 1993), 117-41. "Affection, Cognition, Volition: The Triadic Meaning of Heart in Ethics"
in *American Catholic Philosophical Quarterly* 68 (1994) 211-32. "Nonintentional Affectivity, Affective Intentionality, and the Ethical in Levinas's
Philosophy," forthcoming in *Ethics as First Philosophy,* ed. A. Peperzak
(New York: Routledge, 1994). "The Connaturalized Heart in *The Splendor of Truth,*" in M. Allsopp, ed., *Veritatis splendor: American Responses* (New
York: Sheed & Ward, 1994).

3. See the discussion in the article on SW2 in *The Modern Schoolman,* pp.
153-55.

4. See Bernard Lonergan, *Collection* (London: Darton, Longman & Todd,
1967), Chapter 13, "Metaphysics as Horizon, pp. 202-20. In this re-
view article, originally published in *Gregorianum,* Lonergan uses the
contrast between *Vollzug* and *Begriff,* the act (exercise, performance) of
the intellect and its product, the concept, to emphasize the primacy of
the former, thus preferring Coreth's to Gilson's approach to metaphysics. What sets the limit for consciousness is not our concepts, especially
if the range of sense intuition is taken to be the measure of cognition,
but our intentionality (another name for *Vorgriff*), our transcendence
toward the horizon. Rahner and Lonergan fully agree: our questions
(and our desires, hopes, loves), not our answers, define the reach of
consciousness. If the answer eventually (in "due time") comes from

faith, as hearkening to the word, then philosophy of knowledge becomes philosophy of religion, opening the way for revelation (*Offenbarung*).

5. See the discussion in the article on SW2 in *The Modern Schoolman*, pp. 155-56. See also the discussion in the article on HW2 in *The Thomist*, pp. 921-22.

6. "Illuminating anticipation" is Helen James John's translation, which has the merit of recalling the *lumen intellectuale* without claiming objective knowledge in concepts (light is necessary for seeing but is not itself an object of knowledge, unless made one explicitly), but not without avoiding the usual problem of association with cognition. See her *The Thomist Spectrum* (New York: Fordham University Press, 1966), p. 175.

7. Maurice Merleau-Ponty, *Signs* (Evanston: Northwestern University Press, 1964; trans. Richard C. McCleary), "The Philosopher and His Shadow," p. 175.

8. See Maurice Blondel, *Action (1893). Essay on a Critique of Life and a Science of Practice* (Notre Dame: University of Notre Dame Press, 1984), trans. Oliva Blanchette. See also Henri Boulliard, *Blondel and Christianity* (Washington: Corpus Publications, 1969), trans. James M. Somerville. Also: Jean Lacroix, *Maurice Blondel. An Introduction to the Man and His Philosophy* (New York: Sheed & Ward, 1968), trans. John C. Guinness; see especially pp. 4-37. It should be noted that Rousselot also influenced Blondel, as well as Maréchal; and that among these three there were many mutual influences.

I. The Problem

Chapter 1
Explaining the Problem: Philosophy of Religion as Ontology of the Obediential Potency for Revelation

What do we mean by philosophy of religion? What do we intend when we look for the foundations of such a philosophy? The simplest way of answering these questions is to compare the philosophy of religion with another branch of human knowledge, with which it seems to entertain the most intimate relations—of friendship and of hostility—namely with theology.

Discussing the relations that exist between two sciences looks like a purely academic undertaking. When two sciences extol before each other their autonomy, their dignity, and their loftiness, we have to do with something quite innocuous. We take for granted, of course, that these two sciences exist, that we know what they are. How else should we make sense when speaking of the relations existing between them? There really does not seem to be much to the problem of their [10] relationship.

This, however, is a false impression. When we inquire into the relation between these two sciences, we soon run into a much more difficult problem. What is the foundation of these sciences? What is their nature? And we shall not find an answer to these questions without touching upon some of the most existential concerns of the human person.

Of course, when we begin to speak of the relation between two sciences, we must already know to some extent what we are talking about. We must have some idea of what this science is all about. But this does not mean that we understand its real nature. We may have practiced this science and made great progress in it, yet the *real* nature of its object may continue to elude us and we may be unaware of what the scientific inquiry into the structure of this object *really* aims at. Before it gets to work every empirical science presupposes a law under which it investigates its objects. The fact that very few practitioners of the sciences

are aware of this does not invalidate our assertion. It only goes
to show how natural these presuppositions are and how little
the sciences are aware of their metaphysical [11] foundations.
The data of a science may tell us how it concretely tackles its
objects; they do not tell us what right it has to approach them,
previous to any research, from this particular point of view. The
practice of a science tells us how it works, demonstrates its
method; it does not show us why and for what purpose people
cultivate it.

Logically, if not chronologically, such questions come up
before the practice of a science. They belong to what is called
epistemology or the philosophy of science. They do not constitute a subsequent reflection upon a science; they are an attempt
to justify the way in which each science determines and investigates its object. Since such a philosophy serves as a foundation
for each science, it cannot use these sciences in answering its
own questions. Every particular science rests on a foundation
that is not of its own making, since its very possibility is based
on this foundation.

What we have said applies to all sciences. Otherwise we must
admit that to the plurality of the sciences corresponds a plurality
of heterogeneous principles. But this is impossible, because it
would amount to denying the possibility of the epistemological
question. It follows that there is only *one* philosophical foundation for all sciences. [12] Aristotle had already remarked this in
the fourth book (Chapters I and IV) of the *Metaphysics.* Hence
there exists one branch of knowledge which assigns their objects to the various sciences, determines the structure of this
object, as presupposed by each science, provides the formal principles of knowledge deriving from this structure, and shows how
the existence and the diversity of the sciences follows necessarily from the very fact that they are a human activity. The traditional name of this *epistéme próte* [first science] is metaphysics.
Hence the statement: every problem of the philosophy of science is a problem of the one first science, metaphysics.

Thus we see that the diversity of the sciences is based on a
single, still mysterious ground, which determines their object,
their function, and their differences, and that the problem of the
relation between two sciences is a metaphysical problem. This

does not simply mean that metaphysics may occasionally reflect on the relation existing between two sciences. It means that she herself has originally established this relation, because, as first *epistéme*, she herself gives rise to these sciences. The multiplicity of the sciences must grow out of this one single ground of metaphysics. Therefore the problem of the relation between two sciences does not come up only after they have already been established: [13] it is the problem of the bond that connects them in their common metaphysical ground.

The multiplicity of the sciences underlines the problem of their unity and shows how difficult a problem it is. The same multiplicity allows us to bring out this unity in the clearest and most comprehensive way. It follows that the problem of the relation between two sciences constitutes the most difficult, but also the most profound way of inquiring into the epistemological foundation of each of these sciences. Thus we may say: the problem of the relation between two sciences is basically the problem of the epistemological foundation of each one of them, as both grow out of the same metaphysical ground. By way of conclusion we may say that the epistemological problem of the relation between two sciences is ultimately the metaphysical problem of the one origin and ground that determines their proper object and function and thus establishes between them their specific relation.

Insofar as an epistemological question is also always an inquiry into the nature of science as a *human* activity, it is necessarily an inquiry into human nature itself. We understand a science thoroughly only when we take it not only as a system of ideal statements that are valid by themselves, but as a peculiar human mode of being, the mode of being as those who think and must think these statements. A theory of the human person [14] always implies a theory of the manner in which we ought to act existentially. That is why a problem in the philosophy of science is not merely a manner of satisfying an innocuous curiosity: it concerns our existence as human.

Thus the problem of the relation between the sciences is not only the metaphysical investigation of the basic nature of these sciences, but also an existential inquiry into our very human nature.

What we have said about the meaning of an epistemological problem in general should now be applied to the question that interests us here, that of the relation between theology and philosophy of religion. Let us first repeat what we have established above and apply it to the problem at hand. The problem of the relation between theology and the philosophy of religion is the metaphysical problem of the common ground from which both spring, hence it is also an inquiry into human nature, as the nature of the being who necessarily cultivates these sciences.

This way of formulating our topic brings up a fundamental difficulty, which we may consider from two points of view:

First by confronting the previous knowledge we have of each of these two sciences with our topic as formulated above:

Let us consider what we know about the philosophy of religion. If the Catholic conception of this discipline is correct, we may [15] describe it as that knowledge of the right relation between ourselves and God, between the human and the Absolute, which lies within our reach. A philosophy of religion is supposed to be more than a purely descriptive history or psychology of religion. It depends essentially on some knowledge of God. It is not much more than such a knowledge.

Now for Thomist metaphysics the knowledge of God is not an autonomous science, but an inner moment of general metaphysics, of general ontology. It is neither possible nor necessary to demonstrate this here. The reason is ultimately that "God" is not a fact that may be grasped immediately in itself by starting from ourselves and our experience. For metaphysics, God means rather the absolute ground of all beings and of our knowledge of being, a ground that is always already bared when we inquire about a being as being and which is never known as ground in any other way. As Thomas puts it, God is always given only as the principle of that which is and of our science of it, never as the topic of a distinct, purely human science (see *Spirit in the World*, pp. 327 ff.). Granted this, the following question and difficulty arises: on the one hand, metaphysics is the epistemological foundation of the philosophy of religion as science; on the other hand, the science for which we are seeking a foundation is metaphysics itself, which is supposed to serve as the foundation.

[16] There is only one way of solving this difficulty: the validation of the philosophy of religion coincides ultimately with the self-validation of metaphysics. The problem of the valida-

tion of the philosophy of religion turns into the problem of metaphysics itself. The question about the philosophy of religion becomes the question why we cannot refrain from turning to metaphysics, what metaphysics is and how human metaphysics leads up to God.

Our question grows more difficult if we confront our previous knowledge of theology with our theme as formulated above. Originally theology is not a human work, but a listening to the freely proffered self-revelation of God through God's own Word. In its first and original meaning, theology is not a system of valid statements, set up by human thought, but the totality of the divine discourse addressed by God to us in human language. We can and must then subject it to our own inquiring and systematizing thought and integrate it within the totality of all human knowledge, thus setting up the science of theology. The difference between the first and second stage of theology corresponds to the traditional distinction between positive and [17] Scholastic theology. Scholastic theology, however, is always essentially based upon God's freely proffered self-revelation, upon positive theology, upon the theology that listens.

It looks as though an epistemological validation of this humble listening to and welcoming of God's work were *a priori* impossible, since they presuppose a supremely free initiative of the transcendent God in a self-revelation no human being can foresee. If we start from ourselves, God's revelation cannot be validated either in its actuality, or in its necessity, or in its inner nature. This being the case, we understand at once that an epistemological validation of theology (which should somehow be previous to it) cannot apply to God's word, but only to our listening to it. It can establish that it is *a priori* possible for us to hear an eventual revelation of God. An epistemological validation, previous to theology, cannot expect to do more. And even so, it remains questionable (at least for the time being) whether and in what sense we can discover in ourselves something like a "power of hearing" for an eventual revelation of God, *before* we have in fact heard it, and have thus found out that we are capable of hearing it.

Therefore, whenever we shall speak of an epistemological validation of theology, we shall only mean the demonstration that we are capable [18] of listening to God's message. From the start we are interested not in ourselves as already actually theologians, but as beings to whose possibilities it belongs to become theologians, *if* the free unforeseeable message of God reaches us.

Is it enough for a real theology that the message should reach us as a revealed word coming from without? Or do we need, over and above the power of hearing such a message (a power whose existence may be established by metaphysical anthropology) an inner elevation produced by divine grace, before the perceived message may turn into theology? We cannot discuss this problem here. Catholic theologians are still discussing it. It concerns the importance of the supernatural light of grace not only for faith, but also for a theology based upon faith and its principles. We might, of course, proceed along this line in order to shed light on the whole problem of the relation between theology and the philosophy of religion. It would be the way from above to below, from a study of the believer, influenced by revelation and the light of faith (hence from "theology") to a metaphysical analysis of "natural" humanity, i.e., of the knowledge we possess when we abstract from revelation and the light of faith. In other words: from the totality to a residual part, from theology to the philosophy of religion. This way of proceeding would quite naturally lead us to stress the distinction between theology and the philosophy of religion.

Here, however, we shall proceed in the opposite way: from ourselves and our [19] natural knowledge, not to supernatural theology (we have shown how the very nature of theology makes this impossible), but to an analysis of our capacity of hearing God's revelation, a capacity that makes fully actualized human beings of us. Whether or not we shall succeed in our undertaking will become apparent only as we proceed with our attempt.

This brings us to the *second* difficulty we meet when trying to solve the epistemological problem of the relation between theology and the philosophy of religion. It is a fact that the difficulty increases when we keep in mind and compare what we know already about these two sciences.

We are looking for the one metaphysical ground from which these two sciences proceed; we wish to understand the relation that exists between them, by inquiring into their common root. But how is this possible with regard to these sciences? The philosophy of religion grows out of metaphysics; nay it is metaphysics itself. Is it possible to found theology too on metaphysics? Even if we understand this question only in the sense, mentioned above, of an *a priori*, inborn human power for hearing an [20] eventual revelation of God, the difficulty remains. If metaphysics, as general ontology, when studying the way in which we can know God, establishes the great lines of a philosophy of religion, sets down how we ought to behave with regard to God, must we not conclude that every theology comes too late? Theology is supposed to consist in our listening to the actual revelation of God, as it tells us about our right relation to our Creator. Has the philosophy of religion not told us already about this relation? It looks very much as if the philosophy of religion, as grounded in metaphysics, preempts from the start the function of theology. The real relation between these two sciences seems to consist in the fact that one does away with the other and shows it to be intrinsically impossible. At best a theology of revelation might work out in more detail the great lines that the philosophy of religion has already drawn about our relation to God. Does this not detract from the dignity and autonomy of theology which stands by itself and does not depend on metaphysics?

Revelation is essentially a historical process. That and how it took place depends strictly on a unique combination of historical events, in which God's work has authentically spoken to humanity. The philosophy of religion, on the other hand, seems to be essentially "supratemporal," "transhistorical," exactly like metaphysics with which it is supposed to coincide. Hence the philosophy of religion seems to establish a religion that is [21] basically independent of any historical event, a religion which is equally available to everyone, at every moment of one's existence in history, a religion that may be ever founded again, for which every land is the holy land and every time the fullness of time. For the human spirit can always and everywhere reach the "eternal ideas" of the True, the Good and the Beautiful.

What then do the philosophy of religion and theology have in common? How can both of them together be understood and deduced as distinct sciences from the same common ground? Does our intention of grounding both of them in one metaphysical question make any sense?

Only our study, when completed, can show that this difficulty can be solved. If we tried to solve it right away, we would once more take for granted that we know already what philosophy of religion and theology really are. We have already shown that we cannot know it except by answering the question which faces us. But one point stands fast. We can already say what our answer, if any can be found, is not supposed to do. If the philosophy of religion is to respect the intrinsic autonomy and historicity of theology, it cannot primarily consist in setting up a natural religion. It is not to lay down the great lines that a theology would only have to follow up and to fill out. It has merely to refer us to an eventual revelation of God, a revelation which, if occurring at all, will occur in history. It must not and cannot establish a religion of its own, [22] to be completed or superseded later by a revealed religion. Its very nature demands that it leave to the God and to a possible self-revelation the task of founding and organizing a religion; at least it should never affirm anything without taking such possibility into account.

In other words: Metaphysics, which is already a philosophy of religion, must acknowledge God as the one who is free and unknown; it must understand human persons as beings who, in our innermost spirit, live in history; it must refer us to our history and bid us listen in it to an eventual revelation of this free unknown God. Such a metaphysics will view God as one who is free and unknown, and who cannot be clearly grasped by human groping. It will not make bold to decide *a priori* how this free, personal, unknown God will behave toward us, how and in what guise this God will be and can be revealed, how God will establish the relation between God and humanity. In fine, it will not decide what religion is to be. If such is the stance of an authentic "natural" metaphysics, there is room for an eventual theology, of which metaphysics will be the precursor. Insofar as such a metaphysics views human persons as essentially [23] historical beings, who have to listen for a possible revelation to God, the philosophy of religion becomes the sole possible natural foundation for theology. Thus the philosophy of religion and theology share a common metaphysical foundation and discover their mutual relationship in a question that derives from the philosophy of science.

It is possible by now to state more precisely what we are looking for when we inquire about the relation between the philosophy of religion and theology. We are facing only one and the same metaphysical question: is metaphysics right when it asserts that the human person has to be the being who has to look out in history for possible revelation of the God whom metaphysics makes known to us as the one who is essentially unknown. If the answer is yes, we have discovered the correct conception of the philosophy of religion, we have found the only pretheological way of grounding theology, we have explained the relation that exists between the philosophy of religion and theology in such a way that we grasp the nature of each, the difference between them and their common origin. Here our question about the relation between these two sciences is basically the problem of a metaphysical anthropology which has to view human nature in two different ways:

1) The human person is *spirit*. It belongs to our nature to stand before the unknown God, before the free God, whose "meaning" cannot be determined in function of that of the world or of us. [24] A positive, clear, and definitive relationship between God and us cannot be established by starting from us. God alone can establish it. Thus we must always keep in mind the possibility of a revelation of this God.

2) Even as spirit and precisely as spirit the human person is a *historical* being. Hence it is not only in our biological existence, but also for the very foundation of our spiritual existence, that we have to turn toward history. It follows that from the start, by our very nature, we are oriented toward the historical event of a revelation, in case such a revelation should occur. If, in supreme freedom, God chose, instead of self-revelation, to remain shrouded in silence, we would reach the peak of our spiritual and religious existence by listening to the silence of God.

This will do, for the time being, as an explanation of the task facing us. It consists in laying the groundwork, at least in its great lines, for such a metaphysical anthropology, which may provide us with an answer to our problem, as explicitly stated.

Chapter 2
A Few Related Problems

In the first chapter we have tried to become clearly aware of our topic. To this effect we inquired about the relation between the philosophy of religion and theology. This is an [25] epistemological problem about the relation between the sciences. Such a question does not presuppose a thorough knowledge of the nature of both sciences in themselves. We acquire such knowledge by trying to discover the metaphysical foundation of these sciences, of their object, of the *a priori* principles with which this object must be investigated and of the function that this science fulfills in human life. Only by establishing in this way the foundation of each science in itself, and by showing how both of them, together with their peculiarities and their differences, emerge from one and the same metaphysical ground, can we reach any conclusions about their mutual relationship.

However, when we applied this method to the philosophy of religion and to theology, we encountered difficulties. Our attempt to solve them enabled us to determine to some extent the meaning of our topic and the direction in which a solution might be found.

We discovered that the philosophy of religion for which we are looking is an inner moment of general ontology itself and that it also constitutes a metaphysical anthropology. Within the present context, when we look for the epistemological foundation of theology, we mean only this: we inquire about ourselves as the beings who, in our history, have to hear, or better have to listen to, an eventual revelation of the transcendent, supremely free God. If we want the philosophy of religion to respect the autonomy and the dignity of an authentic theology of revelation, we cannot expect it to establish a [26] natural religion, to decide positively and in detail about our relation to God. It can only consist in an effort to establish, on the basis of human nature, what we called an epistemological foundation for theology. It is an analysis of the human person as the subject to whom is addressed a revelation of God and who is, of our very nature, oriented toward the welcoming of such a possible revelation.

We have thus a first idea of what we are looking for when we inquire into the foundation of a philosophy of religion. In order to shed more light upon our problem, it is good to compare it with similar or contrasting problems. In this way we hope to clarify even further our task and our intention.

Let us first try to compare our procedure with the one that is usual in Catholic fundamental theology. This branch of theology tries to establish scientifically the fact that God has spoken in Jesus Christ. Many problems about its nature and task within the framework of Catholic theology have not yet been solved. As a sequel of the modernistic crisis and right after World War II, the topic has grown alive again. There can be no doubt that it is possible and necessary to find in reason some kind of justification of faith—whereby we use the word "justification" in a conveniently vague way. The utterances of the Magisterium, especially in the XIXth century and when it condemned modernism and every apologetics which uses exclusively the method of immanence, can leave little doubt about the statement.

Fundamental theology usually proceeds as follows: Special metaphysics (natural theology or theodicy) is supposed to have demonstrated [27] the existence of a personal, transcendent God. Next fundamental theology itself establishes the possibility of a revelation coming from God. It demonstrates, at least negatively, that there may exist mysteries that we cannot come to know by ourselves and that may constitute a possible object for a self-utterance of God through revelation. It shows further that it is physically and morally possible for God to reveal such mysteries to us, that this agrees with our human nature, that to some extent and under certain conditions it is even required by it. Finally, this first part of fundamental theology explains that, through prophetic inspiration, God can convey the knowledge of those mysteries to the messengers of divine revelation, and that God can and must, by means of miracles, render the fact of this revelation sufficiently certain and indubitable for us to whom it is addressed.

In its second part fundamental theology tries to demonstrate that such a revelation has actually occurred in Jesus Christ and that it continues to be announced and faithfully preserved by the Magisterium of the Catholic Church.

In this usual procedure of fundamental theology there is one element of an ideal justification of faith that is hardly ever explicitly mentioned. This element is precisely the problem pointed out by the provisional definition of our topic [28].

First, fundamental theology does not spend much time explaining the relation between the knowledge which metaphysics give us about God and the possible content of a revelation. It looks as if the revealed mysteries were added to our natural knowledge as some kind of new knowledge. Of course, we are told that, at least in its innermost core, the content of revelation is a *mysterium stricte dictum* [a mystery in the strict sense]; i.e., a state of affairs so utterly beyond our ken that not only can its existence be known only through a verbal communication of God, but, even after this communication, its inner possibility cannot be positively grasped.

But this does not yet sufficiently explain the relation that exists between the knowledge derived from natural metaphysics and what comes from faith. At first it looked as if revelation meant only that God communicates to us something hitherto unknown to us, so that there simply accrued to us some new knowledge. But when we call the content of revelation a mystery in the strict sense of the word, the contrast between the two kinds of knowledge becomes so great that we no longer see how we might come to know such a mystery. Or, at least, it is hard to understand how such a mystery can turn into the content of our own knowledge, something to which we are intrinsically related, for which we have some kind of finality, at least in the sense that we stand open for the reception of such a revelation.

In other words, fundamental theology does not explain very well how [29], on account of our spiritual nature, we stand open for such a "widening" of our knowledge, how there is room for it in our natural makeup, without having to admit that this knowledge itself is but the necessary fulfillment of our nature. Merely noting that, because of this or that factual reason or obstacle, we are unable to reach by ourselves the knowledge gained from revelation does not remove the difficulty.

Of course, this impossibility might be attributed to the mysterious nature of what is revealed. But this does not totally solve the difficulty. We do not yet understand that and why, of our very nature, we stand open for a knowledge which we cannot reach by ourselves. In other words, we would like to get some insight, from our own side, into the relation that exists between revealed contents and human knowledge.

We might look at the same difficulty from another angle. Traditional fundamental theology does not clearly explain why *a priori*, of our very nature, we are oriented toward such a fulfillment of our knowledge through and only through a free revelation. (This "orientation" does not imply that we have a right to this revelation, but only that we has a duty to accept it, should it freely and gratuitously be granted to us.)

As a rule this orientation is explained as follows. Revelation has in fact occurred. [30] Because of our overall duty of obedience to God we have the duty to obey God's commands, hence, in our case, to accept the divine revelation with faith. However, logically speaking, the metaphysical justification of our duty to listen, to take a possible revelation into account, is previous to the actual occurrence of it. And such a justification remains very formal and general, if it is based exclusively upon our overall duty to obey God. It should be possible to find a more basic, *a priori* justification, one that logically precedes the conviction that revelation has in fact taken place. We should be able to show that, when we appeal to our duty of obedience, as we do with regard to our faith in revelation, such a duty may belong essentially and *a priori* to the necessary forms of human obedience to God and that we can discover this by ourselves. In other words: we must show that listening for a possible order of God, which goes beyond the commands promulgated through creation in the "natural law," belongs *a priori* to human nature. Only if it belongs to our very nature to listen in this way to a command of God, to a command that goes beyond those which, in the natural law, derive from creation itself, can the obedience to an actual command constitute for us a concrete possibility and duty. Only this can lend efficacy to the actual command by which God might impose [31] the duty of believing. This is precisely the topic which we shall have to discuss.

Moreover, the usual fundamental theology pays very little heed to the fact that, by our nature, we are referred to history. Here again we must point out that, before demonstrating any historical fact (thus in fundamental theology the fact of Christ's message, or of his resurrection as the fundamental miracle that anchors our faith), we must show, by starting from human nature, that it is our duty to concern ourselves with such historical truths. Only after having shown in a metaphysical anthropology that it belongs to our very nature, hence also to our undeniable duties, to establish our spiritual existence on historical events and to inquire about such events, shall we have to do with a subject who is willing to accept the proof of a specific historical fact. That is also the only way of thoroughly refuting the difficulty brought up by rationalistic Enlightenment philosophy, for instance by Lessing, that it is *a priori* impossible for a historical fact to come into consideration as the basis of "necessary" truths, i.e., of truths which are essential for human "existence" or human "salvation." To show that Lessing's opinion (as it survives until the present day in all forms of "enlightenment" and of "liberal theology") [32] is totally wrong, that it is not true that historical truths can never serve as the basis for establishing or modifying metaphysical or moral concepts, we must be able to show that, by reason of our very nature, we must turn toward history for the acquisition of metaphysical and moral concepts, which will be concrete enough to serve as a basis for our existence. There is no other way for overcoming modern historical skepticism (insofar as this is possible by mere reasoning). When we are told we must ground our existence on historical evidence, the high regard we have for scientific and technical evidence renders us doubtful or indifferent. We must be shown that human existence is unavoidably founded upon history and that the freedom with which we accept this fact does not detract from any objective evidence, but derives from human nature and the very peculiar object on which we must found our existence.

In fine, it is one of the tasks of a complete fundamental theology to establish that we are fundamentally referred to history as to the domain within which alone we can come into our true nature. Thus we may say that our topic constitutes that part of an ideal fundamental theology that is generally much neglected in practice. We mean the metaphysical anthropology of the human person as the being who, in history, listens to a possible revelation of God.

We are capable of listening to God's message. Let us call such a capability a potency. In our case it is a potency that has no right to demand its object, but that may be addressed by this object and invited to obey its call (*obedientia*). Thus we may speak of that part [33] of fundamental theology that concerns us here as the ontology of our obediential potency for the free revelation of God. In connection with this formula we must note at once that we are not speaking of the obediential potency for *supernatural* life, as our ontic elevation to a share in God's own life, but only of the obediential potency for a listening to an eventual word of God. Should such a word be spoken, we may expect it to occur, at least originally, also within the domain of our natural knowledge, i.e., through human concepts and words.

Our topic is intimately connected with another one that is often discussed nowadays in Catholic theology and philosophy. Both topics may shed light upon each other. We mean the problem of the possibility of a *Christian* philosophy. When we keep in mind the relative autonomy of a philosophy that operates only with the human means of natural reason, we wonder whether there may be something like a Christian philosophy, and, if so, in what sense.

If this timely problem is not, despite all the zeal displayed, to turn into a merely semantic debate about a topic concerning which all parties are in basic agreement, we must say that the "Christian character" of a philosophy consists in this: that precisely as an authentic, as a "pure" philosophy, it refers beyond itself and invites us to assume the attitude of listening to an eventual revelation. Thus it turns into *praeparatio Evangelii* [making ready for the Gospel]. It conceives of the human person as *naturaliter Christianus* [Christian by nature], as one who is ready to welcome revelation. This [34] feature of human nature is not something added to our basic definition merely because a revelation has, in fact, occurred. Without it metaphysics cannot arrive at an original and definitive understanding of human nature. The task we have undertaken is precisely a metaphysical anthropology understood in this way. We may say that it consists in discovering a fundamental justification for a metaphysics that is Christian in the sense explained above.

This is, to our mind, the most correct conception of a Christian philosophy. It does not imply that we remove the boundary between a philosophy that is relatively autonomous in its purpose and method, and a likewise autonomous theology. We want our philosophy to be only a philosophy. Only its own development, of course, will show whether it turns into a *praeparatio Evangelii*, whether by itself alone it refers us beyond ourselves into history and places us before the question of an historical encounter with God. But even in this eventuality philosophy remains pure philosophy, unless one should hold that something loses its autonomy when it is impelled by its own nature to subordinate itself to a higher whole.

The usual interpretation calls a philosophy Christian when it allows revelation and theology to keep it out of error and to enrich it by bringing new problems to its attention. Our conception goes much deeper than this. Keeping philosophy from straying into error, as theology is supposed to do, does not constitute any inner [35] progress for philosophy. Philosophy is apprised of what is certainly false, but this does not help it discover what is true with its own methods. We have our doubts also about an enrichment of philosophy through problems brought up by theology. Such a view seems to overlook too much the qualitative difference between the way theology and philosophy develop their concepts.

At any rate, such a way of being Christian would only amount to a belated baptism of philosophy. A philosophy is Christian in the proper and original sense of the word when, through its own means, it renders itself and so the human person "baptiz*able*," when, under its own steam, it reaches a state of readiness for being *sublated* into the theology that God may possibly establish. We mean "sublated" in the threefold meaning which this word has for Hegel.

First, philosophy sublates itself, i.e., it does away with itself, because it has finished its job, it has exhausted itself in its claim of constituting the best existential foundation of human existence. It is precisely because it assumes and *must* assume this task that it impels us to listen for a message from God and does away with itself as a total explanation of existence. Next, it sublates itself, that is, it lifts itself to a higher level. It reaches this higher level when, as the condition of the possibility for our receiving revelation, it finds its fulfillment on the higher level of a revelation that has really occurred. Finally it is sublated, i.e., it is preserved, because, in the actual hearing of revelation as it takes place in theology, the possibility of hearing a revelation [36] is preserved and has ever again to be actualized.

Summarizing we may say: it is especially when we understand philosophy as the ontology of an obediential potency for revelation that we understand its Christian character, i.e., both its true autonomy and its congenital relationship with theology. This conception of philosophy does not imply that there are not in philosophy plenty of problems that do not so immediately involve any such referring beyond philosophy itself and that, as a result, are at least not immediately relevant for theology.

Should philosophy refuse to accept explicitly for itself this ultimate referring to theology, it would turn into a highly academic, existentially quite irrelevant occupation, because it flatly refuses to investigate the very foundations of human existence. Should it nevertheless insist on baring these foundations, it would become anti-Christian, as it endeavors to present a total explanation of human existence independently of God's revelation. An examination of the usual Scholastic textbooks may show that, despite their orthodoxy and their emphatic allegiance to the Church, their philosophy does not precisely shine out through its Christian character.

Finally we shall mention a third way of shedding light upon our topic. There are two main types of Protestant philosophy of religion which, under many variations, constantly emerge and are still alive today. For the Protestant philosophers of religion (whether or not they go under this name), [37] the content of religion, as expressed in doctrine, worship, and so on, may be interpreted in either of two ways. For the first group it is merely the objectivation of the religious conditions of the human subject, as an experience of value, or a feeling of utter dependence, or an awareness of justification, and so on. For the second group it is the word of the living God as it sovereignly judges all that is finite and human. This word is utterly unexpected. Compared with it all human reality appears as absolute darkness and contradiction, as mere kenosis of the God revealed in and through the godless shadows of everything finite. This is so true that God and this revelation turn properly into the dialectically necessary correlate of humanity's radical godlessness, and that basically nothing can be revealed except God's judgment over everything finite. Thus God is either the inner meaning of the world and of humanity and nothing more. Or God is the one who utterly contradicts us and our world.

The first trend derives from Schleiermacher and Ritschl. It is still alive today and, in the modernistic movement, it tried to invade Catholic theology. It continues to thrive in the history of religions and in its claim that Christianity stands on the same level as all other religions. The second trend is that of the dialectical theology of Barth, Brunner, and their followers. Ultimately, however, these two trends converge into one. Revelation—insofar as this word is or may still be used—is simply something correlative to human nature itself. Only the signs differ. The first trend uses the plus sign: God is the meaning of humanity, nothing more. The other one [38] employs the minus sign: God is the *No* addressed to humanity, nothing more.

With regard to these positions we have a double task. First we must show that God's self-revelation is possible in such a way that this revelation is more than the mere objectivation of humanity's subjective state. This supposes that we cannot by ourselves, in our "infinity," anticipate and reach the absolute fullness of the truth. Next we must show to what extent we possess an inner openness for such a revelation; we must explain that and how, without anticipating its content through our openness we can and must welcome it, if it is proffered. Thus it will be obvious that revelation is not the dialectical correlate of humanity as we remain caught in our finitude. It will be our task to show how there belongs to our essential makeup a positive openness for an eventual revelation of God, therefore for theology, without admitting that the content of this revelation is only the objective correlate of this openness and may be determined by it. This will make it evident that revelation may really be heard without being only the Yes or No to humanity.

After having, in the first chapter, explained the topic of our work and, in the second chapter, compared it with three related topics, our task seems to have been sufficiently determined, insofar as this is possible at the start of our investigation.

[39] We shall look at theology, at the philosophy of religion, and at the relation between them from the point of view of the philosophy of religion, that is, of metaphysics. It follows, as mentioned above, that we shall be capable of shedding light on the nature of revealed theology only insofar as it is possible from this restricted point of view. We view theology only insofar as metaphysics refers beyond itself to something else. We grasp the nature of theology only to the extent that this "something else" is determined by this referring. As we said before, we might have proceeded in the opposite direction and have explained what philosophy of religion is by starting from the conception which theology has of its own nature. But we have opted for the other way.

It may be quite useful nowadays, when there is such widespread skepticism, even among Catholic theologians, with respect to a fundamental theology, to a "rational" vindication of faith, to show that, correctly understood, the philosophy of religion does not in the least endanger the autonomy of theology. Rather the absence of such a philosophy transforms theology (witness the dialectical school) into a philosophy that is bedecked with theology and fundamentally false. If theology erroneously becomes so "autonomous" that it has no more relation to metaphysics, i.e., to human nature as revealed through metaphysics, there is a real danger that it can logically be nothing more than God's No to humanity. All its statements, which have to use human words, can then constitute only a mere No over humanity. They can refer to a divinity, which in itself remains forever unknown, in an exclusively negative way. [40] There can be no more question of a self-disclosure of God for humanity (and not merely for human faith).

The way in which we understand our topic enables us not simply to talk "about" the philosophy of religion, but to present this philosophy itself, by constructing such a philosophy. We do not wish to speak of it as ready-made, but show it in the making.

Metaphysics is difficult when, instead of simply talking about it, we try to build it up. Let the reader not be surprised then if, eschewing what catches the eye, we settle down to some serious work and we assume, as Hegel put it, *die Anstrengung des Begriffs* [the exertion of the concept]. Metaphysics talks always about things which one "always already knows and has known." It is not, like other sciences, the discovery of something one did not yet know, but a becoming aware of what one knew already. Only one who is willing to restrain oneself, to silence the restless curiosity of one's own subjectivity—for it wants right away to be sure of being satisfied—to let the things themselves speak out, may meaningfully inquire what philosophy of religion is, how it stands with regard to theology, why and how the true philosophy of religion is in final analysis nothing but the command given to humanity to listen into history whether God's word has not resounded in it.

Another remark must be made. We are doing metaphysics. But metaphysics is a human science. Therefore it is always and essentially burdened with the incertitude and the obscurity that belongs unavoidably [41] to human nature. Moreover, when individuals do metaphysics, this metaphysics will also not reflect their own restrictions and insufficiencies. Such a state of affairs becomes even more painful when such a metaphysics undertakes in a sense to make room for a possible revelation, for what is divine and divinely certain, or rather to make sure in explicit reflection that this room has already been established by God. But there is no way of avoiding this. We must even expect in our work that, as far as our mere ideas are concerned, we shall construct a receptacle that is too narrow to receive the treasure of the divine faith. Meanwhile we should keep in mind that what we say is the groping attempt to build a scientific conception of the human person in general as a possible subject of faith. We may already possess such a conception of humanity in a provisional and prescientific manner; as believers we are certainly already in possession of it. Therefore, should there be some who get the impression that they cannot agree with all these considerations, this does not mean they would be unable to listen to revelation and to welcome it wholeheartedly. They might consider our attempt an invitation to try to express more explicitly, through their own metaphysical reflection, what they and we know already more adequately by living it in the concrete metaphysics of our existence: a human nature that is basically nothing but a listening to the message of God, that message which, as light and life eternal, leads us into graciously welcoming depths of the living God.

II. The Openness of Being and of the Human Person

Chapter 3
The Luminosity of Being

In the first two chapters we tried to get a first idea of what should constitute the object of our endeavors. Our question is an epistemological one concerning the relation that exists between the philosophy of religion and theology. As such it is a metaphysical question about the common ground from which both these sciences derive an existential question about our nature as those who must practice these two sciences as our characteristic way of existing. We have seen that inquiring in this manner about theology and the philosophy of religion means looking for a metaphysical anthropology in which we understood ourselves as the beings who, in our historical existence, look out for an eventual revelation of God. In order to further clarify this task, we have compared it with the topics studied in the usual Catholic fundamental theology, with the problems of a Christian philosophy, and with the most basic types of present day Protestant philosophy of religion.

From these points of view [43] our topic turned out to be an ontology of humanity's obediential potency for revelation, a proof of the "Christian nature" of metaphysics in the sense indicated above, an overcoming of the opposition between the two fundamental types of the Protestant philosophy of religion, as we established that our positive openness for revelation does not mean that revelation's content becomes an intrinsically necessary and objective correlate of our openness for God.

We may then tackle our next proper task: to draw the great lines of a metaphysical analysis of human nature with regard to our ability to perceive the work of God that may come to us, within the purview of history, as the revelation of the unknown God.

Now, to ask a question metaphysically means to ask it as a question about being. This implies that every metaphysical question must somehow encompass the whole of metaphysics. If such is the case, it is obvious that we undertake our task only with the proviso that it will be enough to draw the major lines of such an ontology of the human person as the possible recipient of a divine revelation. It is quite impossible to do so.

Moreover we must keep in mind that such a procedure continually contradicts the inner nature of a metaphysical investigation. For we have metaphysics as science only where slowly and painstakingly that which is always already known is developed in a systematic and strictly conceptual way, where we try to put into concepts what we have always already anticipated in [44] our being and in our activity. If we make bold, nevertheless, to call the abbreviated procedure that we are forced to adopt, a metaphysical investigation, we feel ourselves entitled to do so only because, in our considerations, we shall, as often as possible, appeal to the metaphysics of Thomas Aquinas. What we cannot do here may be presupposed, because it has been done by him and it may be done with him by anyone who cares to study his works. Yet our task consists not merely in telling what Thomas has thought, because the point of view from which we consider the great lines of his metaphysics, namely the analysis of the human person as a being who can listen to a revelation of God, has not been expressly considered by Thomas.

One aim is a metaphysical analysis of human being. But, as we mentioned above, such a problem includes the whole of metaphysics. Metaphysics is the question about the being of beings as such, it inquires about the meaning of "being." Such is the way in which metaphysics has always been understood and is still, under various disguises, understood today. As human we can never stop, in our thought or in our activity, at this or that reality taken in isolation. We want to know what reality is all about in its unity within which we get to know whatever we know. We inquire about the ultimate foundations, about the one ground of all reality. Insofar as we know every reality as being, we inquire about the being of beings, and we practice metaphysics.

Even when we do not bother asking such a question or explicitly refuse to do so, we still answer the question. We call the question [45] irrelevant or meaningless and have *ipso facto* already given an answer: being is that something which stares at us out of every being as irrelevant, dark, and meaningless. Or we implicitly substitute some particular existent for being as such. It may be matter, or business, the vital urge, or death and nothingness. Every time we make of some reality our be-all and end-all, we make of it the center of everything around us and of all that we are. All the rest is but a means for or an expression of this unique reality. This is the way we say what we mean and wish to mean by being. We are practicing metaphysics. Therefore we must practice metaphysics, since we are always already practicing it. We must ask the question: what is the being of beings?

But every question has a "whence," a principle from which may derive an answer. A question that does not want any answer at all does away with itself. If it wants an answer, it necessarily implies already a certain basis, a well-defined ground, upon which it may and must be asked, whence the answer will have to come. Otherwise any answer would be right, even the most arbitrary one. A question to which any answer at all may be given, is no longer a question. If the answer does not matter, the question too no longer matters, and no answer is expected.

But whence should the universal question of metaphysics about being as such derive its answer? The "whence" of the answer cannot be questioned itself, since it is supposed to constitute the ground on which the answer can stand. But where [46] shall we find the principle of an answer to the question of being in general, since this question questions absolutely everything by questioning what always comes first, being as such? It looks very much as if the starting point for the answer can only be the question itself. Hence the starting point of metaphysics is the question: what is the being of beings? It is this question itself, inasmuch as we necessarily ask it. If we have no right to presuppose that this question is really and necessarily asked by all human beings, then to refuse to ask it, or to admit that we do, would have done away with every "whence" of an answer and made the answer itself impossible.

Thus we have shown that the question about being itself is the solid positive starting point of metaphysics, the premise for every metaphysical answer and statement. Of course, we do not consider only the content of the question; as important at least is the fact that we, the questioners, actually and necessarily bring it up. We cannot abstain [*epoché*] from answering the question about being; an answer is always forthcoming, because the question belongs always and necessarily to our existence. Always and of necessity we posit in our existence the "whence" for an answer, hence implicitly the answer to the question of being itself.

This point is important enough to deserve a few more comments. The question about being belongs necessarily to our existence, because it is implicitly contained in everything we think or say. And without thinking [47] and speaking we are not human. Every statement is a statement about some being. Hence it occurs against the background of a previous, although unthematic knowing of being in general. Every true statement, every judgment, every intentional activity (the activity of someone with "sound judgment," and in every human activity, even when it is "unwise," there still subsists a bit of judgment) contains two components: 1) a synthesis of two concepts, with the claim that this synthesis is correct; 2) the referring of this mental synthesis to "reality in itself," to the objective synthesis of which the mental synthesis is a reproduction. But how can we have access to this "reality in itself," to which we refer the synthesis of subject and predicate of every statement? Precisely through our previous knowing of being as such.

Thomas held similar views. For him too our knowing of being as such does not derive from but is previous to (not chronologically, of course) our knowing of single beings. We are speaking, of course, of our immediate and implicit, not of our explicit knowing of being as such. We advert explicitly to this knowing only in the reflective knowledge of metaphysics.

In fine, whenever we know anything, we also possess an unexpressed co-knowledge [*mitgewußt*] of being as the condition of every knowledge of single beings. This always implies the question what being is, whose co-awareness accompanies all our knowing of and dealings with the single objects of our knowledge and of our activity. The question about being emerges necessarily in human existence.

[48] Thus the inquiry about the being of beings is a necessary constituent of human being and the starting point of every

metaphysical question and answer. Since this starting point of
every metaphysical investigation is characteristic of our being, it
follows that every metaphysical inquiry about being as such will
also be an inquiry about the being of the being who necessarily
asks this question, an inquiry about human being. Hence human metaphysics is also always and necessarily an analytic study
of human being. We may be assured, therefore, that we are not
looking away from ourselves when, at first, we seem to be concerned only with the most general principles of metaphysics.

The metaphysical question about the being of beings as such
is the only possible starting point of every metaphysics. The analysis of this question must tell us about the nature of beings in
general and, in particular, about the nature of the being who, in
its existence, necessarily asks this question about being. We must
accept what follows from this analysis as necessarily as, in all
our judgments and actions, we ask, at least implicitly, the question about being; fundamentally we always also already answer
it. On account of the mutual implication and of the unity of the
question about being and about questioning human nature itself, as they follow from the nature of every metaphysical question, the analysis will always have to be at the same time a general ontology and a metaphysical anthropology.

What is the being of beings as such and [49] in general? We
cannot elude this question; it is a necessary part of our existence; it is our starting point and our only starting point. The
whole of metaphysics is contained in its analysis. The question
has three aspects:

1) It inquires about *all* being as such, not in the sense of the
sum total of all beings in all their multiplicity and diversity, but
in the sense that it inquires about being, which, as one and as (at
least analogically) always itself, belongs to every being.

2) It has to *inquire* about it.

3) It has to inquire about being as such in such a way that
the question aims at the being of being as such, making a distinction between being and beings [*zwischen Sein und Seienden*]
(the many beings to all of which belongs the same being).

There is no need for a long explanation to show that these
three aspects belong to the question about being. We inquire
about being *as such*; it is precisely in this way that metaphysics

differs from all other sciences. They inquire about some domain of beings and from a restricted point of view. Metaphysics inquires about all beings, insofar as they are. It inquires about the being of beings as such. Next, this question is really an authentic *question*. This means: what being is, is always obvious. We know of it [*bekannt*] but we do not really know it [*erkannt*]. Although we know of being, our question is not a rhetorical one. We ask it, because we do not really know what we are inquiring about. Finally, our question always makes a distinction between being and beings. This is precisely what enables us to inquire about being. [50] We know of beings, we know beings, we have continually to do with them, our knowledge refers to them. But we do not know what the being of these beings is. That is why we inquire. This need of inquiring shows in its turn that we necessarily distinguish between being and beings.

We have now to submit these three aspects of the one question about being to a metaphysical analysis, in order to find what this question itself tells us about the meaning of being and about the nature of the one who inquires about it.

In the metaphysical question about being we inquire first about *all* being as such. This implies that the nature of being is to know and to be known in an original unity. We shall call this the self-presence or the luminosity of being. This is the first statement of a general ontology, as it concerns us here. On the other hand, human nature is absolute openness for all being or, to put it in one word, the human person is spirit. This is the first statement of a metaphysical anthropology, insofar as we study it here. In the following chapters we have to establish and to explain these two statements, as they derive from the first aspect of the general question about being.

The nature of being is to know and to be known in an original unity, in other words, self-presence, luminosity. First, when we inquire about the being of all beings, we admit that we have already a provisional knowing about being in general. It is impossible to inquire about something that is in every respect and absolutely unknown. Thus some kind of knowing is asserted [51] and expressed when we inquire about the meaning of being. And since the question about being as such inquires about everything, the knowing contained in it cannot know what it knows as something distinct from what we inquire about. Mysterious though it may be, the being we inquire about is also always already a being we know about. For metaphysics being is all at once the whence and the whither, the beginning and the end of all questions.

Since to the extent and under the aspect that it is inquired about in metaphysics being is always already known, we thereby implicitly affirm that all being is basically knowable or intelligible. A being whose being would of its nature be unknowable is a contradiction. We would be inquiring about it, since the possibility or impossibility of our knowing it is in question. But whence would this inquiry come? We cannot inquire about something absolutely unknown, since every inquiry starts by positing as known to some extent that about which it inquires, and since something absolutely unknowable cannot be known to any extent. The first metaphysical question, the most universal question about being, is already the affirmation of the fundamental intelligibility of all beings. *Omne ens est verum* [Every being is true]. Beings and possible objects of knowledge are identical.

This implies further that every being, as possible object of knowledge, has of itself and on account of its being, hence *essentially*, an intrinsic ordination to possible knowledge and so to a possible knower. For we have seen that intelligibility is asserted as a determination of the being itself. This intrinsic ordination of every being to possible knowledge is an *a priori* and necessary statement. This is possible only if being and knowing constitute an original *unity*. [52] Otherwise this relation of every being by itself to some knowledge might at the most be a factual one, and not a feature of every being, belonging to the very nature of its being. An essential relation of correlativity between two states of affairs must, in final analysis, be founded in an original unity of both of them. For if they should originally be unconnected, i.e., if they were not by their very origin related to one another, their relation would never be necessary, but, at the most, factual and fortuitous. *Non enim plura secundum se uniuntur* [Many things do not constitute a unity by themselves.]

Therefore being and knowing are related to each other because originally, in their ground, they are the same reality. This does not imply anything less than that being as such, to the extent that it is being, is knowing; it is knowing in original unity with being, hence it is a knowing of the being who the knower is. Being and knowing constitute an original unity, that is: to the nature of being belongs a relation of knowing with regard to itself. And the other way round: the knowing that belongs to the essential constitution of being, is the self-presence of being. The original meaning of knowing is self-possession, and being possesses itself to the extent that it is being. Such is the final statement of our general ontology, which derives from the first aspect of our general question about being: the essence of being is to know and to be known in an original unity, which we call the (knowing) self-presence of being. Or, if we wish to say the same thing with a term used in contemporary philosophy: being is self-luminous. Being is of itself luminosity.

This short deduction may become clearer, first if we compare it with the principles of Thomist metaphysics, next if we take care of a possible misunderstanding that may affect this statement and that has in fact affected it in the metaphysics of German idealism. This will provide us with a first idea of the analogy of the concept of being.

First we explain [53] our first statement of a general ontology by means of the axioms of Thomist ontology (see *Spirit in the World*, p. 67 ff.). We have already mentioned the principle: *omne ens est verum* [every being is true]. Intelligibility is a transcendental property of every being. "Transcendental" is used here first in the Scholastic sense of "surpassing the categories." More specifically it means here that intelligibility does not accrue to being from without, or that it does not consist only in a relation, extrinsic to the being itself, to some knowledge that happens to grasp the being in question. Rather it means that the intelligibility belongs intrinsically, from the start, by its very nature to its essential makeup, that it only expresses explicitly what we affirm already when we affirm being itself. Hence, according to this Thomist axiom, intelligibility belongs to the basic makeup of every being. Thus Thomist metaphysics excludes at once all metaphysical irrationalism, i.e., an irrationalism that not only claims that some knowers have no access to all beings (thus denying them the possession of *logos*), but that some domains of being (whether they be called values, life, or anything else) are in principle inaccessible to any logical knowing. *Quidquid enim esse potest, intelligi potest* [For whatever can exist, can be known] (*Summa contra gentiles*, II, 98).

[54] But even for a Thomist ontology this principle is but the way of access to the more essential insight of the original identity of being and knowing in a self-presence, in the luminosity of being for itself, to the extent that and insofar as it is being.

For Thomas the original and fundamental concept of being, hence of knowable object, from which all other objects of knowledge and all other "beings" are but derivations, is actual being, *esse*, or, even less likely to be misunderstood, *esse actu* (being in act). We must keep this in mind, if we are to understand the following statements of Thomas in their real meaning and especially in their universal and fundamental significance and validity.

Thus Thomas emphasizes the original unity of knowable and knowing, which implies more than that one refers to the other. *Intellectum et intelligibile oportet proportionata esse* [The intellect and its object must be proportionate] (not merely proportionally related to each other but) *et unius generis*: they must have the same origin. And Thomas indicates the logical ground for this requirement: *Cum intellectus et intelligibile in actu sint unum* [since the intellect and that which is intelligible in act are one], otherwise we cannot understand how it is possible for the knowable and the knower really to become one in the act of knowing (*In Metaph. prooem.*).

Hence for Thomas being and knowing are also *unius generis*, coming from the selfsame, unique root, in an original unity. Being is *in itself* knowing, and knowing is the self-presence of being, inseparable from the makeup of being. It is the reflection of being upon itself.

Thomas also interprets every instance of knowing, [55] the single act of knowing, in the light of this basic metaphysical conception of being and of knowing. He rejects the popular conception of the act of knowledge as a bumping-into-something, as an intentional reaching outwards. Knowing does not occur *per contactum intellectus ad rem* (*Summa contra gentiles*, II, 98): [through some contact between the intellect and the thing]. If knowing and intelligibility are inner features of being, a single actual act of knowing cannot be understood in its metaphysical nature if one interprets it as a referring of some knower to an object distinct from that knower, as "intentionality." This can, at least, not be the right starting point for a metaphysical understanding of the nature of the act of knowledge. We must rather start from this: that being is of and by itself knowing and being known, that being is self-presence. *Intellectus in actu perfectio est intellectum in actu* (*Summa contra gentiles*, II, 99): the complete ontic [*seins-mäßige*] reality of the intellect is that which is actually known. Since this statement refers to the essence, it is also reversible: in order to be actually known, what is knowable must basically be the ontic reality of the intellect itself. We would totally misunderstand Thomas, our interpretation would be cheap and shallow and reduce his profound metaphysics to something quite pedestrian, if we were to interpret the identity of the knowing and the knowable, which is asserted in this and similar formulas, as if it simply meant that the known as such must be known by some "knower," that the knower as such must know "something," and that in this sense both must be "one." In the statement we have quoted "perfection" means [56] an ontic reality of the intellect as a being. *Idem est intellectus et quod intelligitur* [The intellect and that which it knows are the same thing] (*Summa theologiae*, I, 87, 1, ad 3). *Intellectum est perfectio intelligentis* [what is known is the perfection of the one who knows] (*Summa contra gentiles*, II, 98).

Hence the *species* is not for Thomas something like an "intentional image," but an ontic perfection of the spirit insofar as it is a being. The problem of knowledge distinct from a knower is not solved by appealing to the *species* as an intentional image. Rather for Thomas this word brings up the following problem: how can an ontic determination of a knowing subject, by reaching consciousness, bring about the knowledge of an object distinct from the *species* and from the knowing subject? However, we do not yet have to consider this problem. We have referred here to the correct meaning of species in Thomas so as to avoid the danger of a too hasty interpretation. This might make us unable to understand the real starting point of the whole Thomist metaphysics of being and of knowledge: that knowing, in its first and original sense, is the self-presence of being, that something is known to the extent that it becomes in its being identical with the knowing subject.

We can attempt to summarize our interpretation in the statement: Knowing, in its original nature, is the self-presence of being. Thomas says practically the same thing. What we called the self-presence, is called by him *reditio subjecti in seipsum* [the return of the subject into itself]. For Thomas to know is an activity by which the knower returns into itself, resulting, therefore, in a self-presence. This shows how he [57] basically rejects the popular interpretation of knowledge as what he calls a *spargi ad multa* [a being spread out over many things]. Knowing essentially takes place through the return of the knowing subject into itself; it is coming-to-oneself, a self-presence. Of course this presents the Thomist metaphysics of knowledge with the following problem: if knowing is ultimately a coming-to-oneself, how can a knowing subject ever know anything distinct from itself? It will have to solve this problem (to which we shall return later) without giving up its basic insight into the nature of knowledge. That Thomas considers this coming-to-oneself, this power of self-presence, as the basic constituent of being is evident also from the fact that, in a remarkable chapter of his *Summa contra gentiles* (IV, 11) he claims that the degrees of being—we might say the degrees of possession of being, of intensity of being—correspond to the degrees of the power of coming to oneself, or returning into oneself. A being possesses being to the extent that it possesses the possibility of such a *reditio in seipsum*.

We feel that in this way we have sufficiently shown, within the framework of what is possible here, that in a Thomist ontology there is really room for our first statement of a general ontology: The essence of being is to know and to be known, in an original unity which we have called the self-presence of being, the luminosity of being for itself.

Of itself being is luminosity. Whatever is, to the extent that it is, is not something that may be experienced and [58] known only in obscure urges, in the chaotic turmoil of dark powers. Of itself at least it is luminous; it has always been light. Indeed, being is more than knowing, it is life and action, decision and execution; but it is all this in such a way that all life and action, every decision and execution, insofar as they are (and insofar as they are not, they are nothing), are luminous for themselves, are self-present in knowing, because, although they differ conceptually from knowing, they are moments that belong intrinsically to being itself, to being that is self-present in its luminosity in all the dimensions in which it unfolds its nature.

Chapter 4
The Analogy of Being.
The Knowing Self-Subsistence of the Human Person as Starting Point for a Metaphysical Anthropology

We have elaborated our first statement of a general ontology. Being is knowing, is self-presence. Being has an inner luminosity for itself. We have derived this from the general question about being in its first aspect, in which we inquire about being as such. As a question this question already affirms the intelligibility of being. The essential intelligibility of being, which makes sense only if we affirm the original unity of being and knowing, shows that being means a knowing that returns onto itself, hence self-presence, reflection upon itself, that it is [59] luminous in itself and for itself. Next we have shown how this statement agreed with the basic axioms of Thomist ontology.

Before we continue our investigation we have to consider an obvious difficulty against our conception of being. If being implies the original unity of knowing and of its object, if it belongs to the basic nature of being to be self-present, then it seems impossible that there may exist any being that is not at once knowing and known in identity. But then we have strayed into the basic assertion of the philosophy of German idealism, as it finds its peak in Hegel: Being and knowing are identical. It cannot be our arduous task here to try to explain what this statement implies in German idealism, to what extent it means a deep insight and to what extent a fateful error. Such formulas must always be understood as results of former thinking and must be interpreted in the framework of their historical and philosophical development. Hence it is by no means certain that we have understood this assertion of German idealism simply by stating it. And if it can be understood only together with that what German idealism has deduced from it, it is clear that we cannot go into more detail about its exact meaning. Otherwise we would have to explain the whole philosophy of Hegel. It will be enough here, with respect to this panentheistic thesis of German idealism, to explain *our* statement of the original unity of knowing and being in such a way as to show clearly that it has nothing in common with any kind of pantheism or of idealism (or what is usually known [60] under this name).

We have reached our statement because it is presupposed by the possibility that every being can, in principle, be known. We have shown that this possibility was implicitly affirmed in the first metaphysical question about the meaning of being as such and in general. Hence in order to explain our first statement about the luminosity of beings we must return to its origin, to the fact that we *ask the question* about being. But a question is meaningful only if it is possible and necessary. Possible: that which we inquire about must, in principle, be knowable. Necessary: what we inquire about is not so obvious that it allows of no further questions.

In other words: we can inquire about being only if the question is not from the start and from every point of view made superfluous by an answer, by a complete knowing of the object, only if a question and also an answer (which always presupposes an authentic question) is not rendered impossible by some knowing that no longer allows of any questions. The fact that the question is possible implied that being is self-presence, an original unity of being and knowing. The fact that the question is necessary seems to contradict what we have just said about it. Why should we inquire about being, if it is self-presence, a reflecting upon itself?

If I, the questioner, ask about being, I must be being, since my question shows that I already know about being, and since (according to the first principle of our general ontology) I can know about it only insofar as I myself am what I know. Yet, as inquirer, I cannot be the being about which I inquire, since [61] otherwise, according to the same principle, I should be in unquestioning possession of the being I inquire about. Hence the being that inquires is both being and non-being; its basic inner being is weak; it is not that being to which the first principle of our general ontology strictly applies. The being of the inquirer is not simply and from every point of view the being to which our first principle applies.

On the other hand, this inquirer [*dieses fragende Seiende*] must possess a being [*ein Sein*] to which this first principle applies in some way, since we have deduced the principle from the first metaphysical question about beings as such and in general, i.e., from a question that comprises the inquirer and the inquirer's being. But this makes of the concept of being, to which our first principle applies, a fluctuating concept. We cannot clearly grasp and delimit it. We cannot derive it from any precise statements about its content—i.e., about being as self-presence, as luminosity—by simply predicating being of a being.

The material insight we had first reached, that being is self-presence, self-luminosity, turns into a formal insight: the *degree* of self-presence, of luminosity for oneself, corresponds to the intensity of being, to the *degree* in which being belongs to some existent, to the *degree* in which, notwithstanding its non-being, a being shares in being. And the other way round: the degree of intensity of being shows in the degree in which the being in question is able to return into itself, in which it is capable, by reflecting upon itself, to be luminous for itself.

Hence our first [62] metaphysical principle about the luminosity of being applies only with this restriction: it applies only to a being who is self-present, and constitutes a unity of knowing and being only to the extent that being belongs to it. This extent is intrinsically variable. The same starting point from which we derived our first statement shows us also that we must, in principle, consider this being not as something unchangeable, always and everywhere the same, not, so to speak, as a constant quantity, but rather as a variable function. We have seen that "being" in itself and in the most formal sense cannot be intrinsically fixated. Being is an analogous concept and this analogy shows in the purely analogical way in which every single being returns to itself, can be present to itself. We shall have to apply this finding in detail to human being and to the first and original object of specifically human knowing. In this way it will become even clearer when we shall have to treat of the second and third aspects of our question about being.

At this stage of our investigation we wish to refer once more to Thomist ontology (see *Spirit in the World*, p. 71ff.). Thomas was undoubtedly convinced of the fact that being is the self-

presence of being. However, as a rule, he prefers to express this
basic idea of his metaphysics of knowledge and of being in the
more formal way we have just established. This way emphasizes
that the concept of being cannot be fixated; it expresses at once
its analogical character. *Eadem est dispositio rerum in esse sicut in*
[63] *veritate* [Things are arranged in being in the same way as in
truth] (*Summa theologiae,* I II 3, 7, c.). *Unumquodque est cognoscibile
in quantum est ens in actu* [Everything is intelligible to the extent
that it is being in act] and, on account of the principle of the
identity of intellect and intelligible, we may add at once: *unumquodque est intelligens et intelligibile, quod est idem, in quantum est ens
actu* [Everything possesses intellectual knowledge and is intelligible, which is the same, to the extent that it is being in act] (see
In II Metaph., lect 1, no. 280). *Secundum quod aliquid est ens, secundum
hoc est cognoscibile* [Something is intelligible to the extent that it is
being] (*In VII Metaph.,* lect. 2, n. 1304). And we might add: to
the same extent it is also in possession of intellectual knowledge.

In these and similar statements Thomas affirms two things:
first that the concept of the being of a being is itself a fluctuating
concept, which cannot in its universality be pinned down to a
determined, univocal meaning (hence to a determined manner
of self-presence). Next, that the inner luminosity, the degree in
which being knows itself and is known corresponds perfectly to
and varies with the variability of being. The concept of being is
analogous, as follows from the very starting point from which
we were able to get an idea of what being is; it follows that the
meaning of being, its self-presence, is likewise analogous. Of its
very nature, self-presence, reflection upon itself, is different with
every different being.

We may once more refer to the previously mentioned chapter of *Summa contra gentiles* (IV, 11), in which Thomas superbly
exposes this gradation of the return of the thing into itself,
throughout the different degrees of being. Everything strives
back toward itself, it wishes to come into itself, to take possession of itself, since it is what it wishes to be, namely being, to the
extent that it takes possession of itself. Every activity, from the
purely material up to the inner life [64] of the triune God, is but
a gradation of this one metaphysical theme, of the one meaning
of being: self-possession. Now this self-possession implies a

double stage: an outward expansion, an extraposition of its own essence out of its own ground, an emanation—and a taking-back-again, a reintegration of this essence that has stepped out of its ground and stands as it were revealed. The more these two stages are immanent to the being which steps out of itself and returns to itself, the more a being is able to utter itself and to keep what is thus uttered within itself, to assimilate the uttered essence, so much the more it participates in being, as presence to itself.

Next Thomas examines the different degrees of being. The material being utters itself to some extent in its outward activity, thus showing what it is. But what is thus shown, the manifestation of its ground in its activity, does not stay with it. It is uttered but it cannot be assimilated as such by the one that utters it. It operates only upon others. Strictly speaking it shows only to others what it is and remains hidden to itself. It is no longer luminous for itself, but only for others. It is only in human beings that the utterance of our own essence in thought and in action returns for the first time wholly to ourselves. Insofar as through our thinking and acting we show what we are, we know about ourselves. We "perceive" and "understand" ourselves.

But we cannot enter more thoroughly into these ideas. Suffice it to have shown how for Aquinas too being, self-presence, and luminosity are analogous concepts, which cannot be pinned down, which go through continual inner transformations and which show themselves as such wherever being manifested its nature as presence to itself.

This enables us, in a way that will do for the time being, [65] to reject an interpretation of our first metaphysical principle in the sense of German idealism, as it is generally and rightly interpreted in a pantheistic sense. True, being is knowing. But only to the extent that a being is or has being. Now this being is an analogous concept, analogous for the same reason from which we derived this first principle. Hence not every being is "knowing" or "true" in the same sense and measure. A being is conceivable, indeed it is already asserted as actually existing, that is not an inner moment of a knowledge of the "absolute consciousness." Only pure being is the absolute identity of being and knowing, and perfectly realizes what is meant by the concept of being. In this case of an absolute identity of being and knowing in pure being, in absolute being, there remain no more questions to be asked. The being that is absolute being itself possesses at once in absolute identity, hence in pure luminosity, the object of all questioning: being as such. Hence the question is always already overtaken by an unquestioning knowledge. It is the *noēsis noeseōs* [the thought of the thought].

It belongs to our basic makeup not only that we *can inquire* about being, but also that we *must* do so. It follows that we are not absolute consciousness, but, precisely in our metaphysics, hence *as* "transcendental consciousness," *finite* spirits. Our metaphysical inquire does not imply absolute consciousness. This absolute consciousness does not come to itself in us, not even in our transcendental consciousness. When we feel that we have to inquire about being [66], we show the finiteness of our spirit, in such a way, however, that the question itself reveals that being is, of itself, self-presence, luminosity, the original unity of knowing and being known.

But thus we already anticipate the study of the second half of the first aspect (which will have to treat of human nature) and the second and third aspects of the question about being, the starting point of our whole inquiry about the ontology of the human subject of an eventual revelation coming from the absolute God.

Have these considerations about the meaning of being in general and its basic nature not led us into a field that lies far from our chosen topic? Although one should not expect of a preparatory investigation that its usefulness for the topic proper be always at once obvious even to a cursory glance, it looks as if in our case we have gone back too far before tackling our topic. But this is a false impression. We are in the midst of the most authentic philosophy of religion, insofar as it should be for us a vindication of the possibility of a divine revelation. If revelation is to be the self-manifestation of the absolute to the finite spirit, this presupposes two things: first, that, in principle, every being may be expressed in a "true" discourse, in a communication addressed to the spirit. This is required if we are to speak of the possibility of the communication of a state of affairs hidden in the absolute being. And this (at least this, although there [67] is more to it) is what we mean by revelation. That is precisely what

we have been discussing. The ultimate unity of being and knowing is the ultimate presupposition of the communication of the
ultimate being, of pure being in its "divinity" to humanity through
discourse, through the word. Only if being is from the start
"Logos" can the embodied Logos say in the word what is hidden
in the depths of the Godhead. Only if these depths are not a
dark urge, an abysmal night, a blind will, but eternal light (even
though inaccessible to us left to our own devices) can the word
be the bearer of all grace and of all reality.

That is precisely all we have hitherto not merely asserted in
poetical language, but tried to understand and establish as well
as we could in the exertion of the concept: being, hence above
all pure being, is light and there is no darkness in it. We are
really practicing philosophy of religion in the original sense of
the word.

The second condition supposed for the possibility of revelation is that human nature must possess an openness for the utterance of ultimate being in the luminous word. This openness is
an *a priori* presupposition for the possibility of hearing such a
word. This points to our next task: to infer from the first aspect
of our general question about being what it can tell us for a metaphysical anthropology of the human person as a being who is of
this nature open for a possible revelation.

When, at the beginning of the preceding chapter, we mentioned the three aspects of the general question about being [68],
we formulated the first one as follows: in this question we inquire about being as such, about all being. We must examine not
only the content of this question, but also why we must necessarily ask it. Therefore an analysis of this question is also always
at the same time an analysis of the being who asks it. Thus we
have to make explicit what the first aspect of this question tells
us for a metaphysical anthropology. It tells us this: To be human
is to be an absolute openness for being, or, to say it in one word,
the human person is spirit. The transcendence toward being as
such constitutes the basic makeup of human beings. This is the
first principle of our metaphysical anthropology. We must now
demonstrate and explain it.

We must once more start from the most general question of
metaphysics: What is the being of a being as such and in gen-

eral? We have already shown several times that this question
arises necessarily in human life, so that the answer too, which
this question implies, has to be affirmed with the same necessity.
Above we have briefly established that the general question about
being is necessarily raised in human existence, by showing that
it is implied in every human thought and activity. We must now
once more explain this demonstration in some more detail, so as
to show clearly what relation exists between the knowledge of
being in general, which is already co-posited in this question
and our thinking, speaking and acting, as it occurs in our every-
day life.

We exist in a world of beings that are [69] our objects. We
stand not only in an "environment" as a part of it, as determined
by it; to be human is to have a world, which we oppose to ourselves, from which we detach ourselves, in thought and in action. We "judge" the things, by actively dealing with them. We
do not simply stand in some kind of cognitive contact with the
things of our word, the way we may suppose animals do. We
judge what we know and set it up as distinct from ourselves; we
make the environment of our physico-biological life into our "object," into our world. We do not simply feel and experience our
environment; we pronounce judgments about the world and
about the single objects of which it is made. We are subjects as
against objects. When we know, we do not simply become one
with the other in some neutral ground between within and without, between subject and object. We shall see later that this is
the way the senses know. When we step out of ourselves in grasping the things, we also return so completely into ourselves as
"subjects," as distinct from the things we have grasped in stepping out, that we subsist in ourselves as subjects, as separated,
as opposed to the outside objects we know. In this way what we
experience through our senses turns into objective knowledge
in thought. Thomas calls this return into oneself as subject, with
the ensuing separation of and opposition between this subject
and the sense object the *reditio completa subjecti in seipsum* [the complete return of the subject into itself]. He sees in this complete
return into oneself the characteristic feature of the spirit in contrast with what stands below it.

This human self-subsistence shows in all our activities, [70] insofar as they are human. It shows in the judgment. Every judgment refers something known to an object, refers a predicate to a subject. And insofar as every judgment claims to be true, it intends whatever the predicate refers to as independent from the act of judgment itself. It means the object as it is in itself. In this way, as subject who judges I posit the object of my judgments as distinct from myself, as independent (at least in an ideal absolute order); at the same time, by detaching myself from the object, I oppose myself to it. Thus as subject I grasp myself as standing away from the object of my judgment. In every judgment I know myself as a subject who subsists in myself. And since as human we always think only in judgments (we always think something "about" something, i.e., we judge), the process which we have just tried to describe happens in all our thinking.

This self-subsistence shows also in all human activity, insofar as it is specifically human. Human activity is free. But there can a priori be freedom only where as acting subjects we occupy a position that is independent of the position of the object of our actions. Because in our judgments we return completely into ourselves, thus occupying a position opposed to and independent of the objects of our knowledge, we are free before this object and can freely act upon it. And the other way round: the fact that we can act freely with the things of our world shows that, when we act on purpose, we are self-subsisting in our knowledge and action. Hence this knowing self-subsistence [71] belongs to our essential makeup, and we show and affirm it in every process of our human existence.

What we have said about human thought and activity in general applies obviously also to the judgment implied in the question about being in general. This question too posits the questioned being as existing-in-itself. It is taken for granted that the answer to the question applies to this being as to something independent of the question itself. In the question: "what is the being of a being as such and in general?" a judgment is contained; "It is a being." This judgment is but the most general and formal way of expressing this objectivation of an object in human thought and action, in which cognitive self-subsistence be-

comes manifest. Hence the latter is also always asserted in the
universal question about being. And so we are entitled to ask the
question about the ultimate ground of this cognitive self-subsistence also in connection with the general question about being.

Thus the following problem arises: what is the ultimate reason why we can confront the things with which we deal in our
knowing–judging as well as our free activity with such a power
of self-subsistence? We have explained above how knowing consists essentially in a unification with what is known. How then
must we grasp these things, in our knowing and acting, so that
this grasping, instead of leading up to judgment and freedom,
i.e., to knowing self-subsistence, may not turn into a being-
grasped by the things with which knowledge unifies us? What is
[72] the *a priori* transcendental condition of the possibility of this
self-subsistence?

The answer to this question will allow us to establish and to
explain the above mentioned first principle of our metaphysical
anthropology. Human self-subsistence becomes manifest in the
first question about being, as it necessarily emerges in human
life. It follows that the question of the condition of the possibility of this self-subsistence is one or more element of the analytic
study of what is already implicitly co-affirmed in this first starting point of all metaphysical questioning.

Hitherto our question about human nature has yielded only
a preliminary, rather obvious answer, which we had already no-
ticed, at least from a distance, in Thomas: The human person is
the being, the first being who can perform in consciousness a
complete return into self. This looks like a scanty outcome after
so many words. But we had to emphasize this seemingly obvious fact in so much detail, because it will serve as our starting
point when we explain what we mean when we say that the human person is spirit. This insight will be the first statement which
helps us understand ourselves as possible subjects of a possible
revelation of the divine depths of the absolute spirit who is God.
And that is precisely what we are interested in.

Chapter 5
The Human Person as Spirit

We are facing the question of human being, as it is co-affirmed in the necessity of the general question of being. We wish to know whether and to what extent human being is open for a possible revelation of God. We have seen that being as such is intelligible, hence that it can, of itself, be communicated and expressed, provided only that the one to whom it is expressed can perceive this expression. Thus we come to the problem of human receptivity in knowledge.

In the last chapter we have already seen that, in the most general question about being, as human persons we appear as the beings who, in knowledge, subsist in ourselves, who in judgments and free actions stand in ourselves, and, as such, oppose whatever we know to ourselves as objects. Thus we must inquire into the condition that makes it possible for us, when we know, to stand thus in ourselves and to oppose to ourselves, as objects in themselves whatever we experience. To that effect we must consider in some more detail the peculiar nature of a judgment.

Every judgment affirms a being as such in one of its peculiarities: This is such or such. That is in a sense the most general form of a judgment; it is present also in every action, since here too we have always to do with something that is such or such, of this or that kind. But grasping a single object *as* such or such, of this [74] or that kind, is nothing but grasping the single object of our thought or action under a universal concept. The single object, as given originally in and through the senses, is subsumed under a concept. And this grasping of the single object "under the concept" (the knowledge of the object as possessing the universal quiddity mentioned by the statement's predicate) is but the other side of what we have called the self-subsistence in knowledge of the knowing human subject. For it is precisely because, through our concepts, we as knowing subjects know something of something, because we can refer a universal concept to a *this* to which it applies, that we oppose this *this* to ourselves as our objects and thus reach our knowing self-subsistence. Inquiring about the ultimate ground of the possibility of this self-subsistence is identically asking the following question: what makes it basically possible for us to subsume the single sense object under a concept, to grasp the universal in the singular?

In Thomist metaphysics of knowledge the technical term for this problem is *abstraction*. Abstraction enables us to grasp the universal in the singular, in the particular. It is the condition of the possibility of judging, hence of knowing self-subsistence. We are looking for what makes this self-subsistence possible; we must therefore investigate what makes abstraction possible.

"Abstracting" means "detaching" [*herauslösen*]. When we abstract, we know that the quiddity given in sense knowledge may be detached [75] from the individual thing in which it presents itself to us. It is not of the essence of this "what" to be realized in this and only in this individual object. To abstract means therefore to know that the quiddity given in the individual object is unlimited, in this sense that we grasp it as a possible determination of other individual objects. The whatness (the *forma* or *quidditas* in Scholastic terminology) is grasped as a determination which, in principle, applies to more than this individual object in which it happens to appear and to be experienced through our senses.

This leads us to the question: what is the transcendental condition that enables the knowing subject to discover that the quiddity is unlimited, although it is experienced as the quiddity of one single individual. We are inquiring about the *transcendental* condition of this possibility. That means we are looking for a condition which must exist in the knowing subject prior to any knowledge or abstraction, as the previous condition of their possibility. In Scholastic terms: we are inquiring into the inner nature of the "power" of abstracting. Since in Thomist terminology this power is also called *agent intellect,* we may express our question as follows: what is the nature of the agent intellect?

The power of abstraction is the power of knowing that the quidditative determination presented by the senses in its singularity is, of itself, unlimited. The quidditative determination is first presented to us as restricted to a single sense object. If then we know at once that this determination as such is unlimited, we must somehow [76] grasp that its limitation comes from the single sense object as such. If we are aware of this limitation as such, and as brought about by the "thisness" of the single object, we are also aware of the limitlessness of the quiddity as such.

Now a limit is experienced as such (we do not simply say: we are aware that there is in fact a limit!) when it is experienced as an obstacle to something that wants to get beyond it. Let us apply this to our present case. We are aware that the quiddity experienced in sensibility is limited in and through the single sense object. The fact that we are aware of this limitation reveals to us the limitlessness which belongs to the quiddity as such. This is possible only if the activity that grasps this individual sense object reaches out, prior to this grasping, beyond this individual object, for more than the latter is.

Now this "more" can obviously not be a single object of the same kind as the one whose abstracting knowledge it is supposed to make possible. Otherwise the same question would come up again. This "more" can only be the absolute range of all knowable objects as such. We shall call this reaching for more [*auf mehr ausgreifenden Vorgang*] the *"Vorgriff."* Human consciousness grasps its single objects in a *Vorgriff* that reaches for the absolute range of all its possible objects. That is why in every single act of knowledge it always already reaches beyond the individual object. Thus it does not grasp the latter merely in its unrelated dull "thisness," but in its limitation and its relation to the totality of all possible objects. While it knows the individual object and in order to know it, consciousness must always already [77] be beyond it. The *Vorgriff* is the condition of the possibility of the universal concept, of abstraction. The latter in its turn makes possible the objectivation of the sense datum and so human knowing self-subsistence.

We must explain more clearly what is meant by the *Vorgriff*. It is an *a priori* power given with human nature. It is the dynamic movement [*dynamischen Hinbewegung*] of the spirit toward the absolute range of all possible object. In this movement [*Hinbewegung*], the single objects are grasped as single stages of this finality [*Zielbewegung*]; thus they are known as profiled [*im Vorblick*] against this absolute range of all the knowable. On account of the *Vorgriff* the single object is always already known under the horizon of the absolute ideal of knowledge and posited within the conscious domain of all that which may be known. That is why it is also always known as not filling this domain completely, hence as limited. And insofar as it is *thus* known *as* limited, the quidditative determination is grasped as wider in itself, as relatively unlimited. In other words, it is abstracted.

This is possible only if this *Vorgriff* and the range of the knowable revealed by it is conscious (in a way which we shall have to explain more precisely). Of course, this consciousness emerges only in and with the knowledge of the single object, as a previous condition of the possibility of our knowledge of it. The *Vorgriff* makes us conscious by opening up the horizon within which the single object of human knowledge is known.

We can determine in more detail the nature of this *Vorgriff* only by determining more precisely the range of the horizon which it opens up and in which it posits [78] the single object of knowledge. As briefly mentioned above, it is obvious that this "whither" of the *Vorgriff* cannot be an object of the same kind as the one whose abstraction and objective knowledge it makes possible. For such an object would require a similar *Vorgriff* to be known. Likewise the *Vorgriff* is conscious (otherwise it would have no meaning for our problem). Yet it is not, by itself alone, an act of knowledge. It is a moment of such an act, which, as such, intends a single object.

Nevertheless, although the *Vorgriff* is only the condition of the possibility of knowledge, we cannot help conceiving it (we do not say: affirming it) as some kind of knowledge in itself, because this is the only way we can form an idea of this reaching out of our knowledge to ever further objects. Now, if we must think of the *Vorgriff* as some kind of knowledge, we must be ready to state what the *"object"* of this "knowledge" is. In this sense we ask then what the "object" of the *Vorgriff* is.

We have already said above that this object is the totality of the possible objects of human knowledge, since it cannot be a single object. Such a single object would, as such, also have to be known in conceptual abstraction. How shall we more precisely determine this totality? What is the absolute totality of all possible objects of knowledge, in whose horizon the single object is grasped? It might even be more prudent not to speak of the "totality" of all objects of knowledge, and to ask simply: [79]

whither does human anticipating knowing [*vorgreifende Erkennen*] transcend the single object which it grasps?

There are in the history of Western philosophy three typical directions in which an answer to this question has been attempted: the direction of the perennial philosophy which, in this case, goes from Plato to Hegel, the direction of Kant, and that of Heidegger. The first one answers: the range of the *Vorgriff* extends toward being as such, with no inner limit in itself, and therefore includes also the absolute being of God. Kant answers: the horizon, within which our objects are conceptually given to us, is the horizon of sense intuition, which does not reach beyond space and time. Heidegger says: the transcendence which serves as the basis for man's existence, goes toward nothingness.

It is of course, and unfortunately, not possible, within the scope of these considerations, to investigate this problem and the suggested solutions, in a way that befits its importance. We shall have to content ourselves with outlining very briefly at least the answer of perennial philosophy, as given by Scholastic philosophy. The least we can say is that human knowledge intends what exists, means a Yes. Our problem is to explain how we know about the finiteness of the immediately given object. As long as we can explain this by means of some positive knowledge, of some anticipation which says Yes, which aims at being, and not at nothingness, we cannot and may not interpret transcendence as a transcendence aiming at nothingness.

The only reason why this transcendence toward nothingness might be required is that it renders possible our experience of the [80] intrinsic finiteness of the things and persons that are immediately given to us in knowledge. But the *Vorgriff* toward more than what the single object is constitutes a sufficient and plausible explanation for this negation, for the knowledge of the finiteness of the immediate object of our experience. Nothingness does not come before negation, but the *Vorgriff* toward the unlimited is already in itself the denial of the finite, because and insofar as, as condition of the possibility of knowing the finite, it reveals its finiteness by reaching beyond all the finite. Hence the Yes to what is unlimited in itself makes the negation possible, and not the other way round. So we need not admit a transcendence toward nothingness which, previous to and as the foundation of all negation, would alone reveal the finiteness of a being. The positive limitlessness of the transcendental horizon of human knowledge shows by itself the limitation of all that does not fill this horizon. Hence it is not "nought that noughtens," but it is the infinity of being, at which the *Vorgriff* aims, that unveils the finiteness of all that is immediately given.

Hence our problem can only be this: whether this *more* of the *Vorgriff* implies only a relative limitlessness, as Kant believes, or the absolute limitlessness of being as such, so that the *Vorgriff* opens up a domain beyond the field of spatiotemporal sense intuition. But the former hypothesis contains a contradiction. Not a contradiction between the content of the concepts, as if there were a conceptual and immediate contradiction between the concept "finite" and the concept "totality of the objects of human knowledge." But there exists a contradiction [81] between the act by which the statement is asserted and the content of the statement.

We can know that the totality of the objects of human knowledge is finite only if we reach beyond this finiteness. Otherwise the latter might actually exist, but it would not be known as such. The *Vorgriff* beyond the intrinsic finiteness of the field of human objects, of the domain of sense intuition, which alone can make manifest this finiteness *as* such, would have to aim at nothingness, since, *ex hypothesi*, it cannot reach for the being that is unlimited in itself. Thus Heidegger is the logical outcome of the Kant who opposed German idealism. But the *Vorgriff* toward nothingness is an unverifiable [*unvollziehbare*: unperformable] hypothesis. Thus the presupposition of perennial philosophy is the only one that is possible and that can be experienced [*mögliche und vollziehbare*].

The *Vorgriff*, which is the transcendental condition of the possibility of an object known as object, hence of human self-subsistence, is a *Vorgriff* toward being as unlimited in itself.

Our first and most general question about being is only a formalized way of expressing every judgment, as it underlies all our actions and thoughts. Therefore we may say of every judgment that it contains the *Vorgriff* toward being as such in its limitlessness. Insofar as this question (like judgment and free activity) is of our very human essence, the *Vorgriff* toward being as such in its essential infinity belongs to the basic makeup of human existence.

The same necessity that drives us to anticipate being as such makes us co-affirm the infinite being of God. It is true that the *Vorgriff* does not immediately put God [82] as an object before the mind [*Geist*], since, as the condition of the possibility of all knowledge of objects, the *Vorgriff* itself never represents an object in itself. But in this *Vorgriff* as the necessary and always already fulfilled condition of every human knowledge and action, the existence of an absolute being, hence of God, is always already co-affirmed, even though not represented. The *Vorgriff* co-affirms as objectively as possible that which, as a possible object, may come to stand in its range; otherwise it would once more aim at nothingness. An absolute being would wholly fill the range of the *Vorgriff*. Hence it is co-affirmed as real, since it cannot be grasped as objectively merely possible, and since the *Vorgriff* intends primarily not merely possible, but real being. In this sense we may and must say: the *Vorgriff* aims at God. Not as if it intended God so immediately that it should immediately represent the absolute being in its own self, as an object, and make this being immediately known in itself. The *Vorgriff* intends God's absolute being in this sense that the absolute being is always and basically co-affirmed by the basically unlimited range of the *Vorgriff*.

This is by no means an *a priori* demonstration of God, like that of Augustine, derived from the "eternal truths," or like that of Anselm or of Leibniz. The *Vorgriff* and its range, as the always present and necessary condition of all knowledge, can be known and affirmed only in the *a posteriori* knowledge of a real being and as the necessary condition of this knowledge. Thus the way we understand our knowledge of God is but a translation in terms of the metaphysics of knowledge of the [83] traditional proofs of God, as formulated in terms of the metaphysics of being. Instead of saying: 'This finite being, which I affirm as actually given, demands, as its condition, the existence of an infinite being,' we only say (and we mean the same thing): 'The affirmation of the real finiteness of a being demands as condition of its possibility that we affirm the existence of an absolute being. We do this implicitly in the *Vorgriff* toward being as such, since only through it do we know the limitation of the finite being as such a limitation.'

Once more we must say that it is unfortunately not possible to show in detail how the ideas which we have exposed have been traditionally formulated in Thomism (see *Spirit in the World*, pp. 117-236). We would have to speak of the connection between the "complete return of the subject upon itself" as performed by the human spirit in all its thinking, and the "abstraction," hence between what we have called human self-subsistence and the grasping of the individual sense datum as an object under its concept. Starting thence we would have to show the power of abstraction, what the agent intellect is. It would turn out to be the power of the *Vorgriff* toward being.

The agent intellect is the "light" that permeates the sense object, i.e., puts it within the domain of being as such, thus revealing how it participates in being as such. On the other hand, the actually intelligible object that comes about this way makes that light, i.e., knowing about being as such, in its unlimited extension, emerge into human consciousness. This allows us to understand the correct and profound meaning of the simple sounding statement that the formal object [84] of the spirit is *ens commune* [being in general] and not *ens principium numeri* [spatiotemporal being], and that the spirit is spirit because it grasps everything *sub ratione entis* [from the point of view of being]. This grasping of all objects in the horizon of being as such is often misunderstood. It does not mean that, after we know the single objects, we combine them under a general point of view. It means rather that to be human is to be a spirit because, from the start, in our dynamism toward being as such, we grasp single objects as moments of this unending movement of the spirit [*unendlichen Bewegung des Geistes*]; we see them right away under this horizon of being as such, on account of which we are always already open for the absolute being of God. That is why Thomas can truly say: All knowing beings (he means, of course, those possessing spiritual knowledge) implicitly know God in everything they know (*De Veritate*, 22, 1 ad 1). For Thomas the *concept* of God is that which comes last in all our knowledge. But the *Vorgriff* toward the infinite being is the previous condition of our very first conceptual knowledge, so that in every such knowledge God is already implicitly known. These simple allusions to the way in which our ideas have been developed in accord with Thomist formulations will have to do.

Once more, as we did already in the last chapter, we must ask: Have we not strayed too far away from our theme? And once more we must answer: we are in the midst of a philosophy of religion which, as metaphysical anthropology, has to establish the possibility of a revelation addressed to humanity.

We started with the question: What did our first metaphysical question about being have to tell us, in its first aspect, about [85] the human person as the possible subject of a revelation. The answer has been that it belongs to humanity's fundamental makeup to be the absolute openness for being as such. Through the *Vorgriff*, which is the condition of the possibility of objective knowledge and of our self-subsistence, we continually transcend everything toward pure being. Human beings are the first of these finite knowing subjects that stand open for the absolute fullness of being in such a way that this openness is the condition of the possibility for every single knowledge. Hence there is no domain of being which might lie absolutely outside of the horizon in which we know our objects, and, through this knowledge, we are self-subsistent and capable of freely acting and deciding our own destiny. We call this basic makeup of the human person, affirmed in every act of knowledge and of freedom, our spiritual nature [*Geistigkeit*].

To be human is to be spirit [*Der Mensch ist Geist*], i.e., to live life while reaching ceaselessly for the absolute, in openness toward God. And this openness toward God is not something that may happen or not happen to us once in awhile, as we please. It is the condition of the possibility of what we are and have to be and always also are in our most humdrum daily life. Only that makes us human: that we are always already on the way to God, whether or not we know it expressly, whether or not we will it. We are forever the infinite openness of the finite for God.

A divine revelation is possible only if we ourselves, the subjects to whom it is addressed, offer [86] it an *a priori* horizon within which something like the revelation may occur. And only if this horizon is absolutely unlimited will no law or restriction be imposed from the start on a possible revelation concerning what might and should possibly be revealed. A revelation that is to unveil the depths of Divinity and that is basically the first moment of the invitation addressed to humanity to share in the life of almighty God, is conceivable and possible only if the human person is understood as spirit, i.e., as transcendence toward be-

ing pure and simple. A more restricted horizon of human knowledge would at once and *a priori* drive possible contents of a revelation outside this horizon and render them incapable of being
revealed.

Hence when we state that the transcendence of human
knowledge toward being pure and simple is the basic human
makeup as a spirit, we have made the first statement of a metaphysical anthropology aiming at a philosophy of religion that
may establish the possibility of a revelation.

The knowledge of this transcendence, a knowledge that does
not affirm this transcendence as if it were one human property
among many others, but as the condition of the possibility of our
innerworldy knowing and acting [*innerweltlichen Erkennens und
Handelns*], is the first chapter of an ontology of the obediential
potency for a possible revelation. It is also the essential part of a
Christian philosophy of religion. Being is luminous, it is *Logos*,
and it may be revealed in the word. A human person, on the
other hand, is a spirit and [87] this fact permeates our entire humanity. Hence we have an open ear for every word that may
proceed from the mouth of the eternal. This is the statement that
understands our nature in its very origin and whose meaning
and truth we have tried to understand in the present chapter.

At this stage it is already clear that every philosophy of religion is basically wrong which declares that the object of religion
corresponds to any finite aspect of human nature. No objectified projection of racial peculiarities, of blood or nation, of world
or of anything else, not even the absolute idea of humanity, can
possibly be considered as the "divine." As spirits, human persons have always already transcended all these finite realities
toward something that differs from all this not only in degree,
but basically and in kind. Human persons are spirits and, as such,
we always already stand before the infinite God, who, as infinite, is always more than only the ideal unity of the essentially
finite powers of human existence and of the world. We not only
acknowledge God in fact, but in the daily drift of our existence
we are self-subsistent human persons, capable of judgment and
of free activity, only because we continually reach out into a domain that only the fullness of God's absolute being can fill.

III. The Hiddenness of Being

Chapter 6
The Problem and How to Solve It

Our purpose is to explain the nature of the philosophy of religion by outlining it on the basis of Thomist metaphysics in such a way that it may be seen as an ontology of the human person as the being who, in history, listens for an eventual revelation. From the first aspect of our general question about being, as it inquired about *all* being as such and in general, derived two basic statements. On the one hand, our first statement of a general ontology: The nature of being is to know and to be known in an original unity. We have called this the self-presence or the luminosity of being. On the other hand, the first statement of a metaphysical anthropology: To our fundamental human makeup belongs the *a priori* absolute transcendence toward being pure and simple. That is why a human person is called a spirit. From the first statement followed the insight into the basic possibility of an opening up [*Eröffnung*] of all being in the word. From the second statement the insight that, *a priori* [89] at least, humanity is open for every kind of knowledge and does not restrict the scope of a possible revelation.

The previous considerations may have provided us with a first insight into the possibility of a revelation. But they also bring up a difficulty that seems to militate against such a possibility. We have seen that humanity is the infinity of absolute spiritual openness for being. We have to be this since we are spirits only on account of this transcendence toward being as such. Thus we do not *a priori* put any limits to the possibilities and extent of a revelation through the narrowness of our receptivity, and revelation is not from the start excluded because there is no room within which it may unfold. Now precisely this first statement of our philosophy of religion and of our anthropology seems once more to show that revelation is impossible because of humanity's basic spiritual makeup.

Humanity is the infinity of the absolute spiritual openness for being. In Scholastic terminology human nature is, through the formal object of the human spirit "as it were everything." Does it not look then as if the whole of intelligible being falls within the reach of our transcendental openness, in such a way that the opening up of a divine domain, to which we have no access by our own power, is from the start excluded. Moreover, "theology" speaks of a *new subjective* "openness," through the *inner* light of grace and of faith. This too seems to have become impossible on account of the absolute range of our natural human transcendence [90].*

Since every possible datum lies *a priori* within the reach of human transcendence, the revelation of some datum might at the most mean an actual and merely provisional help. In Scholastic terminology, revelation would be possible only with God's help, but this help would be due to human nature, i.e., to our essential makeup, as we ourselves can know it. Revelation would come from the God of the philosophers, not from the God of Abraham, Isaac, and Jacob. And it should be possible, at least in theory, to transpose every content of revelation into some knowledge that may be deduced from our *a priori* human structure or that is at least due to it. Revelation would only be a propaedeutic to philosophy. In Hegelian terms, it would be the knowledge of the absolute spirit that breaks through in humanity on the level of representation and that develops necessarily into absolute knowledge, in which the finite spirit becomes aware of its unity with the infinite spirit in the form of the concept.

Upon closer examination the same difficulty might have arisen earlier already, from our first statement of ontology, not just from the first statement of a metaphysical [91] anthropology.

---

*As mentioned above, we cannot explicitly discuss this problem here, since it belongs rather to theology or to a philosophy of religion derived from theology. At any rate enough will be said to show that there is still room for a subjective widening by grace of the horizon of human knowledge (a new visibility brought about by the "light of faith" as a subjective faculty, as an "infused virtue"). The only requirement for this (and this is precisely our point here) is that the objective openness of our natural transcendence should not from the start anticipate all possible objects of revelation as due to humanity. [Rahner's only note.]

Speaking very generally, the difficulty consists in this: what we have said hitherto might produce the impression that a revelation, in the sense of the free unveiling of something of itself essentially hidden, is impossible, because in principle every being is always already manifest, and does not need to be revealed. In this event revelation would be nothing else than the immanent and necessary unfolding of this openness of being that is from the start always present in the spirit as such.

We have met this difficulty first when treating of the absolute transcendence of the human spirit as spirit. It looks as if, for the human person as spirit, every knowledge of being is always and in every case but the actualization of our infinite potentiality, hence the necessary unfolding of our own "infinity." The statement of metaphysical anthropology we have established in order to make place for a possible revelation seems to imply too much. It seems to imply the basic idea of the philosophy of religion of German idealism, which—having in mind the semi-rationalism of Günther, Hermes, and Froschammer—the Vatican Council has formulated as follows: "humanity can and must by itself through constant progress reach the possession of all truth and goodness" (Dz. 1808). As mentioned above, the same difficulty seems to arise already from the first statement of our general ontology, at least when taken in connection with the first statement of our philosophical anthropology. If being by itself and necessarily means self-presence, intrinsic lucidity, and reflection-upon-oneself; if being is luminous to the extent that it is being, if it is not being, [92] but only non-being which is dark, then it looks as if being should already always be manifest by itself, at least for that being which is endowed with an absolute openness for every self-luminous reality, i.e., for the spirit.

The highest being, pure being, must always already be manifest for us, at least to the extent that we are spirit and become ever more spirit. Thus revelation would be nothing else than our spiritualization, as it slowly progresses according to the inner law of human nature itself. God would by nature always be the one who is manifest and revealed. Revelation could not possibly be the free activity of God, since divine light always already necessarily shines and illuminates every human person. "Inaccessible light" seems to be a contradiction, because of itself light

necessarily radiates in all directions wherever there is room for
it to shine.

This brings up a problem for a Christian anthropology and
metaphysics. How can they explain human nature in such a way
that, without giving up either our transcendence toward being
as such or the inner luminosity of being, human transcendence
does not anticipate the content of a free revelation? The solution
of the problem will have to show how a free self-manifestation of
the free personal God remains possible despite the fact that this free
revelation can be addressed to a being who is capable of perceiving
it. We shall find the elements of such a solution when we treat of the
second and the third aspects of our initial question.

Since this difficulty derives already from the first statement
of our general ontology, about the luminosity of being, it is our
first [93] duty to look for its solution within this ontology. We
must inquire why, despite and in its luminosity, pure being is
that which is utterly concealed, why being, to the extent that it is
being, is not only present-to-itself, but also hidden, present-only-
to-itself. We must once more go through the transcendental deduction of the luminosity of being in such a way that it may turn
into the transcendental deduction of the presence-only-to-itself,
of the inaccessibility that belongs properly to the eternal light.
We shall further have to take up the same problem in its connection with the first statement of our anthropology.

Our remaining task will materially coincide with the analysis of the second aspect of our initial metaphysical question. This
second aspect emphasizes the fact that in the problem of being
we do really *ask a question*. Not only *can* we inquire about being
(first aspect), we *must* inquire about it (second aspect). This is
the problem we must briefly consider now.

At first sight it might seem as if the infinity of God's being,
as co-affirmed in the *Vorgriff*, suffices to explain why God is essentially the Unknown one for the finite spirit. And since the
finiteness of the human spirit becomes evident, as shown above,
by the fact that it had to inquire about being, the analysis of the
second aspect would be over. It would be enough to say that,
even as a spirit, human nature is finite. The fact that we must
inquire about being, that we feel this need to ask questions, is
sufficient proof of the finiteness of the questioner as such. Our

absolute transcendence as a spirit would reveal [94] the infinite. But this infinity of being stands revealed only in the unlimited range of the *Vorgriff*. Now this *Vorgriff* does not represent the infinite in itself; it only co-affirms the infinite as the ultimate whither [*Woraufhun*] of the unlimited movement [*unbegrenzten Bewegung*] of the spirit we call *Vorgriff*. On the other hand the *Vorgriff* occurs and we know about it only as the condition of the possibility of conceptual knowledge of finite objects. It seems to follow that we know of God's infinity only in connection with *finite* beings.

Thus this infinity would in itself remain unknown to us, since it is grasped explicitly as such only when we deny and reject the finite, the knowledge of which makes the *excessus* (a Thomist term for the *Vorgriff*) emerge in consciousness. If then we know the infinity of God only when, through negation, we move beyond the finite, this infinity seems to be sufficiently unknown, to stand sufficiently unrevealed and shrouded in mystery, so that a new self-manifestation of the infinite remains meaningful and still has something that may be revealed. The fact that we must inquire about being seems not only to exclude any kind of absolute idealism, insofar as it manifests the analogy of being and the finiteness of the human spirit (as explained above), it seems also to manifest sufficiently the essential hiddenness of all positive aspects of the infinite being. This follows from the fact that the reason why we know the infinite, pure spirit, namely, the absolute range of the *Vorgriff*, hence also the infinite of being itself, became explicitly conscious only [95] when we negated the finite being whose knowledge is made possible by the *Vorgriff*.

All this is true and may serve as a first provisional answer to our difficulty. Let us once more go over this first stage of our answer. From the fact that we must inquire about being as such it follows that we know about being as such and about its infinite ground only because we deal with single, finite beings. Hence we may explicitly know the infinite being (*about which* we always already *know* on account of the absolute range of the *Vorgriff*) only by turning toward this finite object and by making explicit the negation necessarily implied in the fact that our intellect always moves beyond it, by negating the finiteness of the finite object. This, however, does not provide us with a positive knowledge of what is beyond this finiteness. The positive aspect of this infinity, which only the concept, not the *Vorgriff* alone, might make known, remains hidden, despite the basic openness of this domain of infinity, which results from the spirit's transcendence. Once more: this first provisional answer is correct. And it is also the only answer given to this problem by the textbooks of fundamental theology.

Yet it does not seem to be sufficient, for the following reasons. What we have said hitherto shows us only that, in the present state of our knowledge, we cannot reach by ourselves a positive knowledge of what is "beyond" the domain of the finite world, although the anticipation of this beyond is the condition of our [96] knowledge of things in the world. But this seems to establish only a *de facto* hiddenness of the infinite being. For we have not yet excluded two possibilities.

The first one is this: We might (or even may) by ourselves reach a stage at which we would, as it were, to stay within our present terminology, become aware of the absolute range of our *Vorgriff* without requiring a finite object as the "matter" in which alone the *Vorgriff* comes to be known as its "informing light." Let us suppose, moreover, that this is the only and highest way in which a finite spirit may get to know the absolute as such, immediately, that God can only be grasped in the *excessus* of the finite spirit (without the intermediary of a finite object, of a finite "image" which represents the object to the spirit). Nevertheless, in such a hypothesis a positive revelation would no longer be possible. We might, by our own powers, be able to reach the highest knowledge of the Absolute. On the one hand, this knowledge would not be merely the usual "negative" theology of rational metaphysics, because the absence of the finite image of a finite object that must be transcended and denied would, from the start, radically do away with the negative aspect of such a theology. On the other hand, it would not be a "beatific vision" in the sense of Christian theology, because this way of knowing God's infinity would occur only in the immediate grasping of the transcendence of the spirit, without the intermediary of any object. If this were the highest knowledge of the Absolute of which we were capable, and capable by our own forces, [97] a revelation of God by God in the word would no longer be required.

This is not a purely arbitrary hypothesis, an intellectual exercise, by which we think of things not absolutely impossible. We believe this represents essentially, as stated in our own terminology, the basic conception of every non-Christian mysticism, expressed metaphysically in Plotinian mysticism, as it continues to exert an undeniable influence upon the Christian mysticism, say, of Gregory of Nyssa or of the Pseudo-Areopagite. The philosophical interpretation of the mysticism of the "dark night" of John of the Cross, as worked out by Baruzi, moves in the same direction.

As a rule, wherever one opposes or seems to oppose "mystical piety" to the "prophetic piety" of a revealed religion, our hypothesis is at work: a mystical experience (usually involving "night" and "ecstasy") in which one reaches out beyond one's finiteness and experiences the infinite, is considered as one which surpasses and supersedes a revelation through the word. To one who has ecstatically experienced God's infinity, a human word, the kind in which God's revelation must speak to us, can no longer convey anything. If our thesis of the absolute transcendence of the finite spirit should end up in a natural mysticism, a revelation through the free word of God would from the start be superseded by a more profound knowledge that one can acquire by oneself. Absolute transcendence might not lead to the absolute philosophy of German idealism (which is to some extent [98] the sober daylight-mysticism of reason), but it would lead to a philosophical mysticism of a "night-ecstasy." Both would have the same destructive consequences for the possibility of a free revelation of God. Mystical piety, even in its simple form of an obscure experience of God in the unlimited infinity of the spirit itself, would have rendered superfluous the prophetic piety of the revealed word with its historical restrictions.

We must further mention a second hypothesis which, if we admit our statement of the absolute transcendence of the spirit, would make a revelation impossible. What we said above about God, that God remains hidden even to human transcendence, would not quite take care of such a hypothesis. Someone might reason as follows: The absolute openness of our human spirit, its dynamic movement [*dynamischen Hinbewegung*] in the *Vorgriff* toward the infinite being, demands the possibility of an immediate

intuition of God as the only definitive fulfillment of the absolute
range of the spirit. Such an intuition might suppose some divine
initiative, but this initiative would simply consist in making possible our natural fulfillment. Each person's natural end as a spirit
would be the beatific vision. The summit of one's spiritual life in
its immanent natural development would not merely be a "night-
like" ecstatic experience of God's infinity contained, as was the
case in our first hypothesis, in the experience of the soaring absolutely transcendent infinity of one's own spirit. It would rather
be the immediate intuition of the essence of God's infinite being
itself, as given in itself. This would lead us very near the hereti-
cal position of the mysticism of the Begards: "that every [99] intellectual nature is naturally blessed in itself, and that the soul
does not need the light of glory to raise it to the vision and the
happy fruition of God" (Dz. 475).

       We cannot reply to this hypothesis that the question of
whether or not the beatific vision is due to humanity or only
bestowed upon us as a grace has nothing to do with the question
of the possibility of a revelation, since these two questions treat
of quite different things. This is precisely not the case. If
humanity's natural end is the beatific vision, which unveils God's
essence more than can be done by any possible revelation in mere
words and in finite signs, we can no longer conceive of a revelation as a supremely free act of a God as a free and gratuitous
self-manifestation. At most it might still be conceivable as a verbal anticipating disclosure of a God who is at least in principle
always already the final goal of the human spirit.

       To this objection we may give the following answer, which is
undoubtedly important and fundamental: We have admitted the
absolute range and limitlessness of the human spirit's transcendence as a condition of the possibility of an objective knowledge
of finite beings and of human self-subsistence. The purpose of
this transcendence is to make possible the peculiar mode of being which turns a finite being into a spiritual being. This purpose has been reached even when the capacity of this transcendence is never immediately filled by the manifestation of the infinite being itself. We have posited and we were able to establish
this transcendence *only* as the condition of *this* possibility. We
have not presented it as a function that had its own *telos* [end]

for itself alone. Hence we have no right [100] to demand that
this transcendence should, in itself, independently of the makeup
of our human spirit, receive a fulfillment other than the one on
account of which we affirmed its existence.

In a philosophical anthropology we know only of a human
knowledge that demands, as a condition of its possibility, besides the *Vorgriff* toward being as such, also the representation of
a finite object, to render the *Vorgriff* conscious. It follows that
philosophically we cannot say whether the spirit's transcendental capacity may ever be filled without the help of a finite sense
object. We cannot say whether the beatific vision is intrinsically
possible, much less whether it is humanity's due.

Once more: all this is true and must be taken into consideration. But our conclusion that the beatific vision cannot clearly
be assigned as humanity's natural end does not yet prove that it
is essentially supernatural and utterly undue to humanity; it does
not prove that, despite our absolute transcendence, God continues to stand before us as the one who is still unknown, and that
in this way there remains an object for an eventual revelation.
And we might even wonder whether human nature as such, i.e.,
"by nature," has received its finality toward the infinite for no
other purpose (even if this is the only purpose for which we can
show that it has been given to us) than to roam forever, a per-
petual wanderer, through the domain of the finite, in order to
greet the Infinite always only from afar, without ever discovering the direct road that would lead us before the face of God.

Thomas himself speaks of a natural [101] desire for the immediate intuition of God. It is not quite certain what Thomas
meant exactly by this expression. Every theologian who has
written about it seems to have an interpretation. At any rate, it
shows that Thomas admitted that there are, between our spiritual nature with its immanent dynamism (its *desiderium*) and the
beatific vision, relations that do not merely derive from the fact
that humanity has been called by grace to the immediate intuition of God, but that are previous to this invitation and rooted
in human "nature."

What we have just said about the difficulty deriving from
the natural possibility of a beatific vision applies also, *mutatis
mutandis*, to the difficulty arising from the hypothesis of natural

mysticism. It is impossible to demonstrate positively the possibility of such a mysticism, as interpreted above, at least not in a deductive metaphysical anthropology, whose only starting point is the nature and the function of transcendence. Such a transcendence has a purpose and a meaning even if such a mysticism does not or cannot exist. On the other hand, what we have said hitherto does not allow us positively to exclude such a hypothesis.

Thus we have not yet discovered a final answer to our question: why does the absolute transcendence of the spirit as the *a priori* opening up of a space for revelation, combined with the pure luminosity of pure being, not from the start render superfluous any possible revelation?

We have merely reached the following conclusion: Humanity stands before God as before one who is at least for a time unknown. For God is the Infinite, whom [102] we can know as infinite only by denying the finite and referring to that which lies beyond any finiteness. This referring is the condition of the objective knowledge of finite realities.

If known in this way, God remains hidden in the positive content of divine infinity. But is it not possible that God remains hidden simply because humanity does not yet know God, because we, as finite spirits, have not yet reached the end of our spiritual movement [*geistige Bewegung*]? This has not yet become clear. Hitherto we have explained the fact that God remains hidden only by studying humanity, more specifically the merely factual structure of our spiritual being. Thus we have explained it more through our blindness than through God's intrinsic inaccessibility. We shall understand the possibility of a divine revelation as a free act of God only if we can establish that God remains essentially hidden before every finite spirit as such, and not only before humanity in the actual structure of human knowledge. It is not enough for us to know that God is more than what we have hitherto grasped of God in our human knowledge, as we get to know it in an anthropology. We must also know that God may speak and may refrain from speaking. Only then can God's actual speaking to us, if it really happens, be understood for what it is: the unpredictable act of God's personal love, before which we fall upon our knees in worship.

Chapter 7
God Free and Unknown

When taken together the first two steps of our ontology and anthropology have made place for a possible revelation. Being is luminous by itself. Human nature is, by itself, at least insofar as the range of our transcendence is concerned, capable of taking up in our knowledge every possible reality. But this leads us to a basic difficulty: does an absolute transcendence facing a being who is pure luminosity not make every possible revelation superfluous? The last chapter has explained the difficulty and established a few truths important for its solution. On account of the finite character of our knowledge, and despite the absolute, limitless range of our transcendence, God remains forever the unknown one, so far as the actual knowledge of the human spirit is concerned. Moreover, it is impossible to demonstrate that the immediate vision of God is humanity's natural end.

But this does not altogether answer our question. Even so it is still conceivable that God, as God, might always still be the one who is already manifest. Thus we have not yet established the possibility of a revelation as a free self-examination of God. Yet, from the point of view of a philosophy of religion, only this kind of revelation explains the fundamental autonomy and the heterogeneity of theology with regard to every philosophy. The philosophy of religion turns into a possible theology only when this point has been clarified.

[104] Thus we start again with the second aspect of our general question about being. We do not know what being is, while knowing what it is. Insofar as we can and must inquire about being as a whole, we are always already by anticipation [*vorgreifend*] present to being as a whole. Thus we always already affirms this luminosity of being as such.

Why do we affirm this intrinsic luminosity of being as such? Is it because we are bathing in the light of being as such? Does being as such by itself immediately reveal its intrinsic luminosity to us? Should this be the case, God's absolute being should di-

rectly manifest itself to us. It is only in this way that we might
know immediately about the luminosity of being as such in an
objective evidence of being as such, i.e., through a self-manifestation of being. But if we contemplated absolute being in its own
luminosity, it would be impossible for this being about which we
can inquire, whose luminosity we thus affirm, to be at the same
time and as originally the being about which we *must* inquire.
The answer would so thoroughly have anticipated the question,
that the latter would be no longer possible. This consideration
radically excludes an ontology and a philosophy of religion based
upon ontologism and upon its disguised twin, rationalism. We
have already mentioned that, in this context, a philosophy of
religion along the line of German idealism, is impossible.

But how can we then explain more precisely the necessity of
affirming nonetheless the luminosity of being [105] as such? We
cannot see it in the absolute being. Neither can we, by simply
examining the content of both concepts ('being' and 'intelligibility') discover that they are essentially connected when applied
to being itself. In fact, when we deduced the first statement of
our general ontology, we have already mentioned the reason of
this necessity.

We must explicitly affirm that we know enough about being
to inquire about it, since we affirm it implicitly in the question
about being, as it arises unavoidably in human existence. To be
able to abstain from inquiring about being would be not to have
to affirm the statement that being is intelligible in itself. But in
every human judgment and activity there is some knowledge
about being as such. Thus the question is always implicitly raised:
what is being that we always already knows by anticipation, whenever we deal with individual beings in our thinking and activity.

Thus the evidence of metaphysics is based upon the necessity revealed in human existence. The last metaphysical evidence
available to us is not a material but a formal evidence. It is not
the material evidence of an insight into being as such, which
would be an insight into absolute being. It is the formal evidence
rooted in our human necessity of being what we are: the beings
who inquire about being in our every thought and action, who,
while we inquire about being, and despite its basic hiddenness,
have always already affirmed that we know it enough to inquire

about it, that it is luminosity. We can affirm this only insofar as we affirm our existence and because we have to affirm it with its own human characteristics. Being as such essentially opens up for us when, as it cannot refrain from doing, [106] human existence takes possession of itself.

Human existence, which permeates in this way the insight into an ultimate necessity, is a purely factual existence. It is contingence, thrownness [*Geworfenheit*], to use Heidegger's term. To deny this fact would be a denial of human finiteness. It would amount to an endeavor to put humanity in the very midst of being, as it extends into infinity before human transcendence. It would do away with humanity's need to inquire about being. Thus we must assume our existence in its mere thrownness, if we are to be human existence, i.e., if we are to stand before being's luminosity which we necessarily affirm. Hence the first metaphysical affirmation of an absolute necessity is at the same time the affirmation of human contingency and thrownness. Only by resolutely assuming our own finiteness and thrownness do we find access to being's true infinity.

What follows from this? We have discovered the starting point for a new basic insight in our general ontology (which always includes also a statement about God) as well as for our metaphysical anthropology. Our next task is to develop this new insight as regards general ontology.

Once more we start from the peculiar structure of human existence as we have come to know it from all our previous considerations. In our self-subsistence and in the objective nature of our thought and activity we develop necessarily an attitude toward ourselves. We must necessarily be [107] present to ourselves, affirm ourselves, posit ourselves absolutely. On account of this necessity we inquire about being as such, and insofar as we inquire within this necessary acceptance of our being, we know about being as such. We affirm the luminosity of being and our own transcendence toward being as such and in this way we stand before God.

Insofar as we must *inquire* we affirm our own finite thrownness; insofar as we *must* inquire, we affirm it necessarily. And as we affirm it necessarily, we affirm our existence—in and despite its thrownness, as unconditioned, as absolute. In other words:

because the affirmation of the *contingent* fact is unavoidably *necessary*, the contingence itself reveals something absolute: the unavoidable way in which the contingent fact demands to be affirmed. Despite its contingency it excludes the possibility of being denied. This implies that humanity necessarily assumes a relation of absolute affirmation with regard to our finite and thrown [*geworfenen*] existence. It is only in this necessity of a conscious relation to the non-necessary that we transcend toward being that is luminous and affirmed as such.

Now to posit something contingent absolutely is to will. Such a positing must intrinsically be more than a mere static insight; it must be will. Mere conceptualizing as such can derive the ground of its affirmation only from the object itself. Now something contingent as such does not have in its *quidditative* essence any ground to be absolutely affirmed. If its present existence itself is considered as the ground for affirming it, for positing its quiddity absolutely, this existence would be posited as necessary, since only such an existence can be the ground of an absolute affirmation. [108] Hence this existence would be the necessary existence of something contingent, which would be a contradiction.

Hence the affirmation of the contingent does not simply find its ground in the object as such. The ground is thus first the ground of the act of affirmation, and only afterwards the ground of the object as affirmed. But such a ground is called will. Therefore in the ground of human existence we discover within the primordial transcendence toward being the (necessary) act of the will. The fact that being opens up for human existence is brought about by the will as an inner moment of knowledge itself. We must now first examine this knowledge in the direction in which it includes a statement about being itself, hence in the direction of general ontology. The next chapter will consider what it can tell us for metaphysical anthropology.

We have seen how the fact that we will ourselves is a condition of the possibility and of the necessity of the question about being and so a condition of our knowledge of being as such. What follows hence for the nature of being, especially of pure being, and for its relation to finite beings, especially to finite human existence?

At the basis of human existence is always enacted [*sich vollzieht*] a necessary and absolute affirmation of the contingent reality that we ourselves are, i.e., will. It always goes together with an affirmation of the luminosity of being as such. It follows that this necessary volitional affirmation can only be conceived as the ratification [*Nachvollzug*: re-enacting] of a free absolute positing of something that is not necessary. For should this absolute positing of contingent [109] human existence not originate from a free will, the basic luminosity of being as such would be eliminated.

In that case, the *necessary* positing of something contingent, which is known to be contingent, hence not to be posited absolutely, can only derive from a ground that is dark, not luminous for itself, not aware of itself. For let us suppose that we as human, the contingent reality that is being posited, should derive from a ground that cannot not posit us. Then we have the choice between these two hypotheses: human being, the reality posited, is as necessary as the act by which it is posited. Or the positing cause is of such a nature that any attempt to clarify it, by means of a "logical" connection between it, the act of positing, and what is posited, would be frustrated by the peculiar nature of the cause. But both hypotheses are unacceptable. The former, because what is posited is contingent. The latter, because being, the positing cause, must in final analysis be luminous, and because the connection between a necessary act of positing and a contingent, not necessary object of this act, can never be made luminous.

It follows that the voluntary *necessary* positing of something contingent, as it occurs in the affirmative relation of human existence to itself, can only be understood if we affirm it as posited by a *free* voluntary act. Humanity is necessarily posited, because posited by a free will. We necessarily posit a contingent reality absolutely while in the same breath affirming the luminosity of being. This makes sense only if, by doing so, we ratify and endorse the act by which this contingent being has been freely and voluntarily posited as absolute. This free, voluntary, original [110] positing of the being that is humanity (for we are thinking of ourselves in all our considerations) can only be the work of the

absolute being, of God. We have already mentioned above that
God must be affirmed as the universal ground of all that is. Here
our purpose was only to show that this positing of the finite being by God must be an act of free will.

This implies that in our necessary and absolute relation to
our thrownness as it affirms the luminosity of being, we affirm
ourselves as a freely willed effect of God. We know that our
being is carried by the *free* power of pure being. It follows that
we do not stand before pure being, the final horizon of our *Vorgriff*, as if it were a lifeless [*unbeweglichen*] ideal which, always at
rest, must always be available to our grasp; we stand before it as
before a subject of free self-disposition. God is the whither of
the *Vorgriff* of the human spirit, but is such because God looms
before the finite as free power. Thus, when finite knowledge
knows God, this knowledge is carried by God's own free positing of this finite reality, which we call creation. Thus it is always
already a reply to a free word, spoken by the absolute, implicitly
affirmed as such a free action when, on account of our transcendence, we finite spirits perceive the distant radiance of the infinite light.

Central in this whole discussion are the following points: As
spirits who know the absolute being, we stand before the latter
as before a freely self-disposing person. And this personal face
of God is not ascribed to God because we belatedly [III] provide
absolute being with human features. Rather God appears as a
person in the self-disclosure [*Sicheröffnen*] of absolute being for
human transcendence, because absolute being appears in the totality of being about which we not only can but must inquire.

When in our knowledge we meet a free, autonomous person, our knowing slips back into an unknowing. Because of freedom, persons manifest of themselves only what they wish to manifest. In the case of the free positing of something that is not necessary, there is no previous *a priori* whence it might be known. It
can be known only by and from itself. Insofar as the free positing of God makes God appear to us as a person, the knowledge of
this personal God depends always on God's own free decision.

Thus humanity always stands already before a God of revelation, before a God who operates in history. For if, from the
start, God appears to human transcendence as the free power, it

takes only two more conditions to make God known as the God of a possible revelation: 1) the possibility for divine freedom to bring something about must not be exhausted by the creation of a finite being who is capable of knowing God. In other words: God's creative possibilities must not have come to an end with the creation of humanity. God must still have further possibilities of free activity [112] with regard to this human creature; 2) this creature must still have a capacity for the knowledge of such an additional free operation of God with regard to itself. In one word: there must still be room for the object of a further free activity to be known by a knowledge that has not yet reached its limit.

Now both these conditions are fulfilled. The free creation of the finite and the contingent by God implies already as such that God's further activity with regard to this creature cannot be simply and altogether the logical consequence of God's first creative action. The contingency of this finite creature implies as such that it is changeable, hence that by itself it must be the object of further possible free interventions of the absolute. Since the creature depends wholly on God's free will, it cannot unfailingly tell us about the direction of God's free activity. The second condition is also fulfilled. The horizon of possible beings opened in the spirit's transcendence extends in principle beyond everything that is not the immediate vision of God's absolute being. We have already said that this vision cannot be shown to be the connatural end of the spirit's absolute transcendence. Hence as long as this vision is not granted to humanity there remains room for accepting further divine communications that God may freely deem fit to bestow.

Therefore insofar as, in our absolute and not wholly fulfilled transcendence, we stand before the free God, our first question about being (a question that characterizes us as human) puts us before the possibility of a free activity of God with regard to us [113]; hence it puts us before the God of a possible revelation. Now a free activity is always unpredictable, hence final and unique. Therefore such a revelation is not simply the continuation of the manifestation of being that would already, although only inchoatively, have started for us in its definitive and final direction with our natural knowledge of God.

In order correctly to evaluate the scope of these considerations we must keep in mind what follows: They do *not* intend to
demonstrate that there exists in the depths of God mysteries that
belong to God's necessary essence (for instance, the Trinity) and
are, nonetheless, essentially mysteries, i.e., accessible to us only
if God's grace freely reveals them to us. They intended to show
only that, through transcendence, as it occurs in us in its human
form, we do not merely stand before the absolute being as *semper
quiescens* [always at rest], but before the God for whose free activity with regard to us there still remain actual possibilities and
in us the power of knowing them. Will this God enter in contact
with us and how will God do it? Can God thus make known
mysteries of the necessary divine essence, mysteries in the strictest
theological sense? We shall not try to answer these questions
but leave this task to the *a posteriori* knowledge that derives from
the actual revelation of this God.

But for our purpose the following insight is of the greatest
import: Human transcendence toward the being that is absolutely luminous and totally intelligible is at the same time at least
the openness for a God who can act freely with regard to us [114]
in a way we cannot discover by ourselves. Hence the transcendence toward pure being is a standing before the inscrutable
mystery whose way cannot be investigated and whose decisions
cannot be probed. If such is the case, the knowledge of God as
the absolute being implies that we must consider the possibility
of a divine activity that goes beyond the free creation of the finite spirit.

This is enough for our purpose. For in that case to be human
persons is essentially always already to be those who listen for a
possible revelation of God. Since at the same time and for the
same reason that we stand before God, we stand also before the
God of a possible revelation, there always occurs something like
a revelation, namely, the speaking or the silence of God. And we
always and naturally hear the word or the silence of the free
absolute God. Otherwise we would not be spirit. Our being spirit
does not mean a demand that God should speak. But, should
God not speak, the spirit hears God's silence. Otherwise we
would not be spirit, since we would not stand before the living,
free God as such. As spirit we stand before the living, free God,

the God who speaks or the God who keeps silent. That is why, on account of our innermost nature, we cannot remain indifferent with regard to an eventual revelation of the living God.

If there were no danger of being misunderstood, we would like to say this: By our very nature as spirit, we always hear a divine revelation. Metaphysically speaking, [115] revelation is simply the free activity of God which, as such, is always and necessarily a manifestation of God's essence, beyond the manifestation included in the nature of the finite spirit and what follows from it. When persons face one another as free beings, they always manifest themselves, precisely as the persons they wish to be in regard to others: as a person who keeps aloof or as someone who opens up. In this sense revelation occurs necessarily. And since in this sense revelation occurs necessarily (we do not merely say: might occur), humanity must necessarily take account of revelation in the usual theological sense: of a possible word of God that breaks divine silence and manifests God's depths to the finite spirit. It is precisely because revelation, in the above metaphysical sense, occurs necessarily and because we are always affected by it, that revelation in the theological sense is free. For revelation in the theological sense does not consist in God's opening up to us or not, but is the actual opening up of God's hidden essence. We may, of course, not say of a revelation in this sense that it is necessarily granted to us on account of our nature. On the contrary, it is essentially free.

Thus we have once more, starting from the fact that we have to raise the question about being, carried out the transcendental deduction of our being as that of a being who stands before the self-present, luminous being of God. We have seen that to be human is to face the free and inscrutable being of God, hence the God of a possible revelation. Despite its intrinsic luminosity and despite the absolute transcendence [116] of the finite spirit, pure being is the most inscrutable, because in its transcendence as mere transcendence (questionability), it appears as supremely free. The first statement of our general ontology was: Being is presence to itself. Its second statement is: Pure being is free being, hence it is not from the start and necessarily manifested to the finite being.

Chapter 8
The Free Listener

We are trying to carry out a metaphysical analysis of human nature, with a view to a philosophy of religion that would be an ontology of the human person as the subject of a possible revelation. A metaphysical anthropology is always also at the same time a general ontology, otherwise it would not be metaphysical. Thus our analysis of human existence always speaks also about being in general, and in particular about absolute being. Such assertions of general ontology are always important for the philosophy of religion as well.

The first statement of our general ontology said that to the extent that being is being, it is presence to itself, luminosity. It follows that pure being could not contain anything that, because of its absolute "irrationality," was unable to be expressed in the word of a revelation.

The first statement of our metaphysical anthropology said that the human person is [117] spirit, i.e., we posses an unlimited transcendence (openness) for being as such. Hence it belongs to our innermost nature to stand before God; and the range of our possible knowledge does not, from the start, include a law which excludes *a priori* the possible disclosure of certain objects.

In the preceding chapter we have once more conducted the transcendental analysis of our general questions about being, starting from the fact that we must raise the question about being. We wished to find out what insight this would provide for a general ontology. We came to the following conclusion: Pure being is always already known not only as the final whither of our absolute transcendence, but also as the supremely free will that carries the finite beings. It manifests itself freely and personally by freely acting upon its creatures. This free and personal manifestation has not come to an end with the creation of the finite spirit.

Thus the absolute being is, despite and in its openness for the transcendence of the finite spirit, a reality that is in itself inscrutable, that freely manifests itself or keeps silent, as the God of a possible revelation through a divine word, the God of a necessary revelation through word *or* silence. Standing before God, the basic attitude of human existence is always at bottom a standing before the free God in the still unfulfilled and incalculable possibilities of divine freedom, and thus a standing before the God who acts in history, before the God of revelation. Thus we came upon the second statement of our general doctrine of being (a statement about the [118] absolute being): before the finite being, the absolute being is the free being.

We must now answer a further question: What does the analysis of our general question about being under its second aspect tell us about *our* nature? It is quite natural to expect that the problem of general ontology discussed in the preceding chapter has something to tell us about this nature.

As human we are the beings who, as finite spirits who inquire and must inquire about being, stand before the free God, affirm our freedom in the way we raise the question of being, and must therefore take this divine freedom into account. Because of this freedom God can manifest a personal countenance and reveal the divine nature in a way that cannot be discovered *a priori* in some other manner. These findings of the last chapter gave us several data for an analysis of human nature.

In connection with them we have also discovered that there occurs, at the core of our finite knowledge of being, especially of the absolute being, a necessary voluntary affirmation of our own thrown existence. Being opens up for the human spirit through and in a voluntary attitude toward itself. Not in the sense that our knowledge of being should be preceded by a blind impulse and volition, resulting in a dull unintelligibility and only afterwards giving rise to some knowledge or to a "spirit" that would remain imprisoned in its dull origin without ever being able to make it translucid. This would be a shallow and wholly false interpretation of the important insight that has been brought up as a presupposition of our previous findings.

[119] This insight has nothing to do with a metaphysical irrationalism, except for the kernel of truth that is necessarily contained in such a false conception. When we established that, in knowledge itself, there is a voluntary element, we have only said

what is evident for a Thomist ontology: that being is always spirit and will, true and good, that knowing is being and that it is knowing only as being, so that it cannot be adequately grasped in its *own* essence, unless it be also grasped as will. It follows that willing is not *merely* an inner aspect of knowing; it is also at the same time a transcendental determination of being, one that proceeds in a certain sense *beyond* knowing. But this is another problem, which we shall not examine here, although this idea was already germinally present in the last chapter.

This insight into the voluntary moment of knowledge as such is the starting point for our further investigations. For this and for other reasons it is important to see this point clearly. Therefore we now once more come back upon it.

Our considerations ran as follows: As humans we necessarily affirm the luminosity of being because we necessarily assume an affirmative stance toward ourselves, as we necessarily are present to ourselves in object knowledge and in action. We necessarily assume an affirmative stance toward ourselves, because, even when in thought and in action we say No to ourselves, we still affirm ourselves as being, because in the very act of such a [120] denial we still presuppose ourselves as possible objects of such an act, hence as being.

But in such a necessary attitude toward ourselves we affirm ourselves as finite, as thrownness [*Geworfenheit*], as contingency [*Zufälligkeit*]. Insofar as we affirm ourselves necessarily, our existence is, despite and in its contingency, something unavoidable for us, something we have to take up, in that sense something absolute. Despite its contingency it is not submitted to the decision of the finite being, to our choice between Yes and No; it raises an absolute claim to affirmation; it demands to be accepted and despite its thrownness it has always already imposed this affirmation.

In this irresistible acceptance of something contingent, of a double possibility that has already been decided in favor of one side—which presents us with a free choice, and thus does not justify, or "make luminous" the choice as it favors one side—we affirm in the transcendence at work in this choice the luminosity of being as such. How is this possible? Something is luminous when it is intelligible. But the contingent seems to be basically unintelligible. We say that something is intelligible only when it is grasped in connection with its ground, when it is, as it were, replaced onto its ground and viewed as emerging from it as its necessary consequence. Our statement about the intelligibility of being in itself derived from the fact that, always and also in the first question about being every possible object of knowledge is already viewed by anticipation under the general aspect of being as such. Hence there can be no being that does not, by itself, positively range itself in the context of being as such.

[121] This is precisely the reason why it is intelligible. Something contingent that would, in its mere contingency, stand loose and unconnected, in absolute isolation, would not possibly, on account of its being, range itself within being's totality. And it is precisely this connection with being's totality that makes the particular beings intelligible. Therefore such an entity would be basically unintelligible. But this contradicts the first general statement of our ontology. Hence the term intelligible must be reserved for either absolute being itself, because, as the whither of the human *Vorgriff*, it causes the spirit's openness for the totality of its possible objects, or for the single finite being that is object of knowledge when and insofar as it is grasped as grounded in this pure absolute being. Otherwise this single being would have no ground of its intelligibility, since the latter means that something stands within the absolute horizon of the possible objects of knowledge. This is the case only if either this being itself constitutes the absolute horizon of knowledge (as a finite being it is unable to do this; it does not fill this horizon), or it must be grasped as connected with the objective horizon of knowledge. It must have its ground (the ground of its being, of its intelligibility, of its being ranged within the horizon of being as such) in the absolute being. We have made clear enough in the last chapter that this standing of the finite reality, its being grounded in absolute being, must be conceived as voluntary and free.

We must now take up again more thoroughly our previous considerations. It is possible, after what we have said above, to reconcile the contingency of human [122] existence, which we must necessarily affirm, with the luminosity of being as such? At first it looks very much as if the unintelligibility, i.e., the fact that the single contingent being could not be ranged in the context of being as the totality of the possible objects of knowledge, had simply been displaced from the contingency of that being itself to the contingency of the act that posited it, from contingency to the contingent fact of God's freedom.

First we must admit that, even when we are given such a ground of its being posited and of its intelligibility, the posited reality remains unintelligible for us in the contingency. For we see the act of creation only in what has been created. Hence for us, who do not see directly the free act of creating, this act remains as dark as what has been created. However, we are not trying to reconcile the contingency of the finite being with *our* finite knowledge of being, but with its luminosity, which belongs to it in itself.

The question is now whether, in its free creation by God, the contingent itself is luminous? Is the free act of creation itself (as distinct from what is created) not once more something unintelligible, since a free act as such has no reasons that determine it, and thus explain it and make it luminous? In other words, does the free God understand God's own free action? Or does that action, in its "contingency" and its "groundlessness", stand before God as something unintelligible?

It is clear at once that this question cannot and must not be answered in such a way that the expected luminosity of the free act would jibe with a concept of intelligibility that would arbitrarily have been set up before our question had been answered.

Since we are still busy [123] with our first explanation of the general question of being, we are still trying to find first of all the right concept of the luminosity of being that is supposed to be the essence of being into which we are inquiring. We must try to reach this right concept of being's luminosity by starting also from the freedom of the act. Thus we are entitled to reverse the question and to inquire: How should the luminosity of being be understood so that God's free activity may be understood as luminous in itself?

Basically knowledge is self-presence of a being in its being [*Beisichsein des Seienden in seinem Sein*]. Hence where the self-presence is complete, knowledge too is complete. When a being has totally taken possession of itself [*Besitznehmen von sich selbst*], the essence of knowledge has also reached its fullness. Now, a free act is originally not so much the positing of something else, of something external, of some effect which is distinct from and opposed to the free act itself. It is rather the fulfillment of one's own nature, a taking possession of oneself, of the reality of one's own creative power over oneself. Thus it is a coming to oneself, a self-presence in oneself.

The action is free and cannot be deduced, but it is not something that faces the one who knows it *in the very act of performing it* as something other than in its contingency. It is, at bottom, the agent itself. That is why it is luminous for the *agent*, even though it may be dark for *another* who is present only to that which is performed and not to the performing itself. The fact that the free act belongs to the innermost meaning of self-subsisting being shows at the same time that it is most intimately luminous for the free self and dark for all others.

This act [124] is most perfectly self-present, hence it is something that is most luminous in and for itself, something also that is least accessible to others: light for itself and darkness for another. It can become luminous and understandable for another only when that other co-performs [*mitvollzieht*: co-enacts] this act as free act, when the other loves it.

Hence the free action is luminous in itself. And if it seems to be dark and unintelligible, it is so only for a knowledge that tries to understand it while standing outside of it. But this does not detract from its intelligibility. It is only an invitation extended to knowledge to work itself, as it were, into the free activity in order to understand it and its effects. This happens when one tries to understand the free action of the other not after it has already been carried out, but when one takes part in the performing itself, or, by ratifying [*Nachvollzug*: re-enacting]it, lets it, as it were, emerge also from oneself. In this emerging itself the free activity may be present to itself, i.e., it may be understood.

We may note in passing that the concept of luminosity, which we have already mentioned before this chapter, where we explained it in function of freedom, shows that freedom and intelligibility may be reconciled. Above we explained intelligibility as the possibility of ranging a reality within the totality of possible objects, either because it is pure being itself, the last whither of all efforts at understanding, or because it is ontically connected

with this pure being. This way of explaining what is intelligible
shows that a free act of pure being itself is at once intelligible in
itself. We have, however, avoided this shorter road in behalf of
the opposite [125] procedure, from freedom to luminosity, because
it provides us with new insights that are important for us.

To start again where we left off, the finite has its ground in
the free, luminous act of God. But a free, self-present act is love.
For love is the luminous will willing the person [*gelichtete Wille
zur Person*] in his or her irreducible uniqueness. It is precisely
such a will that God sets in action in creating a finite being. It is
God's way to exercise will in free, creative power. Thus the contingent is understood in God's love and only in it: the finite contingent being becomes luminous in God's free love for self and
for what God freely creates. Thus love is seen to be the light of
knowledge. A knowledge of the finite that is not willing to understand itself in its ultimate essence as reaching its own fulfillment only in love, turns into darkness. It must erroneously consider the contingent as necessary, or leave it in its absolute unintelligibility, an unintelligibility that does not exist and that knowledge steadily denies; or it must explain being as a dark urge, in
whose depths there shines no light. For the finite may be grasped
only when it is understood as produced by divine freedom. Now
God's free action is luminous for us only when we do not merely
take it as a fact. We must also ratify [*nachvollziehen*: re-perform,
re-enact, identify with, actively unite with] it in our love for it,
thus experiencing [*erleben*] it, as it were, in its origin and its production. Thus love is the light of the knowledge of the finite and
since we know the infinite only through the finite, it is also the
light of the whole of our knowledge. [126] In final analysis, knowledge is but the luminous radiance of love.

Hence insofar as God, in self-love, freely loves as the creator of the finite, God understands the finite itself in this love. In
this light the thrown is also raised to the light of being. Because
and insofar as God loves the finite, it shares in the luminosity of
pure being. There is for it no other way of sharing this light.
Only in the logic of love does logic reach the understanding of
free being.

However, our purpose was not simply to shed light upon
some obscure points of our previous considerations. We wished

to inquire into the being of the human person, as it looks to us from the second aspect of our question about being. We are making progress in this direction.

We have already said that the necessary welcoming of our own existence could, on account of its thrownness, be understood as the continuation and the ratification [*Nachvollzug*] of its original free production by the absolute being. It has thus become clearer why, in this transformation of pure knowledge into knowing love, the absolute affirmation of the contingent becomes so luminous that the affirmation of something contingent in God's knowing love does in no way contradict the luminosity of being. This provides us also with some insight into the ratification of this affirmation by us. It is a ratification of the self-luminous power of God's supremely free love, which is basically God's self-love.

This means that at the heart of the finite spirit's transcendence there lives a love for God. Our openness toward absolute being is carried by our affirmation of our own existence. This affirmation is a voluntary attitude of ours with regard to ourselves and, in final analysis, [127] a reaching out of finite love for God, because, as will of the spirit, it can affirm the finite only as carried by God's self-affirmation. This implies that our self-actualizing [*sich vollziehende*] standing before God through knowing (which constitutes our nature as spirit) possesses, as an intrinsic element of this knowledge, a love for God: our love for God is not something that may happen or not happen, once we have come to know God. As an intrinsic element of knowledge it is both its condition and its ground.

In the previous chapter our analysis of the fundamental nature of the human person has shown that we are the beings who stand before the free God of a possible revelation. We stand there through a voluntary (even a necessary) attitude toward ourselves. We see now that this attitude is based on an attitude toward God. So if we wish to think our anthropological analysis through to its end, we must inquire what follows for it from the mutual relation between willing and knowing as the two inseparable components of the one basic human structure, as we stand before God.

The opening up of the transcendental horizon of being as such, which makes us stand before God, takes place in our voluntary attitude toward ourselves: the human re-enacting [*Nachvollzug*] and taking effect [*Auswirkung*] of the free positing of this finite knower is through God. In the heart of knowledge stands love, from which knowledge itself lives. We do not mean that knowing [128] is *preceded* by a blind urge. Rather knowledge and love constitute originally the one basic stance of the one human being, so that neither can ever be understood except as a turning into the other, as grasped in function of the other.

To come back very briefly to a Scholastic formula, we might say that we have only developed the meaning of the Scholastic axiom: "being-truth-goodness are convertible." We might, of course, also say: "being-intellect-will are convertible." This amounts ultimately to saying: Even while maintaining the conceptual distinction between them, we must conceive of knowledge and of will as essentially intrinsic elements of being and of each being insofar as it is being. Thus something is knowledge only to the extent that it is being. Being is something only to the extent that it is also understood as will, so that knowledge too may be understood in its fullness and in its origin only when it turns into will, so as to reach the fulfillment of its own nature in the total makeup of a being (that is also will). Will and knowledge can only be understood in a *reciprocal* priority with regard to each other; their relation is not a one way affair.

We have hitherto always spoken of this voluntary attitude, entailed by the spirit's openness, as being necessary. We necessarily have an attitude toward ourselves. In this dynamism of self-assertion we affirm ourselves. We must now have a closer look at this necessity.

This voluntary self-affirmation, which occurs in the [129] transcendence toward being as such, is necessary in this sense that it cannot be avoided. It should not be confused with a blind, dull fate, with some kind of metaphysical inertia. It is a form of understanding. We affirm ourselves *as* something because our affirmation, although implicit, happens consciously. Thus this self-affirmation may be necessary in its occurrence without having to be necessary in the concrete manner of this occurrence. Because this self-understanding is a *conscious* [*wissendes*] one, its necessity is not of such a kind that its concrete manner is fixed once and for all. We necessarily understand ourselves in some way. But the *way in which* we concretely assume an attitude toward ourselves may nevertheless depend on our original freedom. Again this does not mean that we might understand ourselves in the full autonomy of our decision about ourselves, as if the way we understand ourselves were wholly left to our choice.

The necessity of our self-affirmation implies already a directive that tells us how we must understand ourselves. All that we have hitherto said of human nature was but the explanation of this directive. But even so, this self-understanding is, in the way it happens, an act of human freedom. We must show why this is so.

Insofar as the things given in human knowledge are grasped through the *Vorgriff* in the horizon of being as such, they are known as objects of a self-subsisting subject. Insofar as this transcendence happens within a voluntary attitude, these objects are grasped as possible goals of a voluntary attitude, of an [130] affective [*emotionalen*] decision, i.e., as values. This means that being itself is grasped as a value. Thus the human person is the absolute transcendence toward the absolute value, which is pure being, God. Above all, this absolute value is not given as object, but only as the whither of the *Vorgriff*, which is always also will. To put it in Scholastic terms, we know it only as "beatitude in general," not as an object; it is given only as the condition of the possibility of our grasping a finite value.

We have seen that, in the line of knowledge, the spirit, through its transcendence toward absolute being, objectifies the finite reality whose finiteness it knows, and grasps itself as self-subsisting. Likewise in the awareness of values, the spirit, in its transcendence toward the absolute value, knows of the finiteness of the single value that it encounters and knows itself as actively self-subsisting with respect to such values, i.e., as endowed with freedom. In the affirmation of a value it is subject to necessity, and in this sense not free, only to the extent that the affirmation belongs to the conditions of the spirit's necessary openness to value as such. Only this *a priori* condition is necessarily affirmed, together with what is implied by it (and only insofar as it is immediately such a condition).

Before single values, insofar as they are given in our representations, we are free, because values are always represented as finite (although not necessarily affirmed as finite). In this way we are also free with regard to the conditions of the possibility of our openness to value as such, if and insofar as they become, in our reflection, objects of knowledge. [131] This makes it possible to understand suicide or hatred for God, although implicitly we continue to affirm ourselves and the absolute value, as the conditions of the possibility of our negative attitude with respect to our own existence and to the absolute value. As *objects* they are not conditions of possibility and that is why we can be free with respect to them.

What is the relation between this possibility of human freedom with regard to values and our necessary affirmation of the right order of values, as implicitly contained in the transcendence toward being and value and thus belonging to our basic makeup?

We may first reply that there exists more than some kind of logical agreement or opposition between this necessarily affirmed correct order of values and the order of values implied in the free choice between values. Of course, some such agreement exists and it is the first point we have to mention here. Love for God, which is necessarily present deep down in human existence, may be explicitly welcomed by us in our free activities, or the latter may contradict it, exactly as a single judgment may agree with the first laws of being and of thinking, or may stand in contradiction to them.

But this is not all, nor is it what matters most. Rather it is a fact that the free decision about single values (among which belongs also the decision about the absolute value as objectified by our reflection in our *a priori* openness to values) has a repercussion upon our fundamental openness for the right order of values. This does not mean that this openness could be altogether [132] destroyed. But a free decision about a single value is ultimately always a decision about and a molding of oneself as a person. In every decision we decide about ourselves, not about an action or a thing. Thus in our free decisions we work back upon ourselves; we affect the very criteria of our love, which determine our own being. To the extent of our power and of what is possible, we set up, in our free decisions about single values, in what we accept and in what we reject, the criteria of our possible further decisions. We not only *assume* the structural laws that govern our love and hatred, but we ourselves freely *display* [*setzt von sich aus*] anew the right laws, which we always already welcome unconsciously, or we set up our own laws in opposition to the right order of love. Thus we do not merely string out without any connection single actions one after the other. But in every action we set down a law of our whole activity and life. We do not simply perform good or bad actions: we ourselves become good or bad.

In this way we construct, above the true order of love, which we always implicitly affirm (the ancient philosophers called this *syntheresis*) our own order of love. We know and act according to our self-chosen order, according to what we ourselves have freely decided. We can behave according to the right order of love only after having rendered it explicit before our minds. That is why we know this order, as established by God, only in combination with the freely constructed order of our love, which we have [133] rightly or wrongly set up through our free reaction to single values.

At this point we must remind the reader that, within our transcendence toward God, there stands our voluntary attitude toward ourselves. Thus some love is the condition of our knowledge of God. Of course, we have first said this about our necessary love for God, that is always already given with human existence. Now, however, we see that in our free activity this necessary love is never present by itself alone, as some "pure" love; it is always combined with the order of love we freely set up, which may agree or disagree with it.

This implies that our concrete transcendence toward God always contains, as one of its intrinsic elements, a free decision. The free decision does not merely follow from knowledge; it also influences the latter. It follows that the deepest truth is also the freest truth. The way we know and understand God is always also carried by the order or disorder of our love. We do not first know God in a "neutral" way and afterwards decide whether to love or hate God. Such a neutral knowledge, such "objectivity" is an abstraction of the philosophers. It is real only if we suppose that our concrete order of love is correct, that it agrees with the necessary order of love, which comes from God and rules in our innermost being. The concrete way in which we know God is from the start determined by [134] the way we love and value the things that come our way.

Metaphysical knowledge never meets its object in itself, but comes to know it only in function of the subject's own transcendence, of our dynamism toward this object. Thus such metaphysical knowledge can never be evaluated in function of the object itself; moreover, it depends on all the concrete peculiarities of this transcendence. This by no means detracts from its strictly objective and logical character. But such knowledge always is commitment of the whole person in a free decision. A change in this knowledge is, in this domain, always also at the same time a "conversion" [*Bekehrung*], not merely a modification of one's opinion or the result of some investigation. Thus we all have the God who corresponds to our commitment and to the nature of this commitment. If we love matter more than the spirit, we will adore it as the absolute, as our god. If we center the understanding of our nature around the vital urge, we will—to speak metaphysically with St. Paul—make our bellies into our god. And so forth.

The truths that all people admit, those of mathematics for instance, are not demonstrated more certainly or more strictly than those of a metaphysics of God. But they are admitted by all only because they belong to our surface (that of numbers and space) and thus can never contradict the basic option contained in our understanding of being as determined by the way we freely love. Metaphysical knowledge may be demonstrated in a stricter and more consequent way, because our innermost being always necessarily co-affirms it. But what [135] is thus co-affirmed can become the object of explicit knowledge only to the extent that this knowledge fits in the structure of the love for which one has opted in one's concrete conduct. The fact that it is possible clearly to establish for a scoundrel a mathematical truth, but not a proof of God's existence, demonstrates neither the strength of the former nor the weakness of the latter. It only goes to show the extent to which a demonstration needs one's personal commitment.

Ascetics may be understood in the sense of a readiness to criticize one's own order of love and to evaluate it in the light of the remainder of this order as it subsists in everybody and to organize it ever anew and more correctly in the growing light of true insight. In that sense it constitutes an intrinsic component of the philosophy of the real person. This truth has practically been totally overlooked in the philosophical activity of the later centuries, with results we know only too well. Only one who, in spirit, lives in temples and cloisters, can be a philosopher.

What follows from this for our philosophy of religion? We had already said that we are the beings who stand before a free God and before the still unfulfilled possibilities of divine freedom, hence before the God of a possible revelation in the sense more precisely explained above. We have now advanced one step further and shown that the openness of human knowledge for this God of an eventual revelation, which belongs to our basic human makeup, is always at the same time and essentially an openness which, in its inner concrete structure, is determined by our free attitude.

[136] We have seen that the openness toward God is a question of one's moral self-determination. When we consider the knowledge of God as a real event in a real person, we see that it is intrinsically a moral or rather (since it refers to a decision with respect to God) a religious problem. Thus we may formulate the second statement of our metaphysical anthropology as follows: To be human is to be that being who stands in free love before the God of a possible revelation, to listen for God's word or God's silence to the extent that we open up in free love for this message of the word or of the silence of God. We hear this possible message of the free God when we have not, on account of a wrongly directed love, narrowed the absolute horizon of our openness for being as such, when we have not, in this way, made it impossible for the word of God to say what it might please God to say, to tell us under what guise God wishes to encounter us.

These considerations are but an attempt to understand philosophically what the Lord has said: "Whoever does the truth comes to the light." God's light is absolute brightness and likewise humanity in itself is the unlimited receptivity for all light. This was the conclusion of our first stage, of the analysis of the general problem of being under its first aspect. God's light is free light. That is why, in and despite its absolute brightness, it shines for the finite spirit in the way it pleases. Thus its shining is not simply the expansion of a natural process, but the action of a free love. Basically the human person is the absolute capacity [137] which, in and by itself, does not narrowly restrict God's light. But at the same time, in and precisely because of this absolute capacity, we are the free ones, who decide about ourselves and thus makes up our minds whether and to what extent we wish to hear the truth and to let God's light shine in our spirit. Such is the conclusion of the second stage of our investigation, of the analysis of the question of being under its second aspect.

We still have to answer the question: What is the concrete place where the free possible revelation of God can encounter us who know in freedom? If we are the beings who must always look out for God's free action, through which God will eventually be manifest, where must we look in our existence so that we may encounter it if it should take place or has already taken place? This is the further question which we must try to answer.

IV. The Place of the Free Message

Chapter 9
Explaining the Question

We finished the last chapter with the following question: Where in human existence is the concrete spot where, as the beings who listen for a possible revelation of God, must we stand in order to hear it, should it actually occur or have occurred? In what direction do we turn to listen for the possible coming of a revelation of God or to be struck by the silence of God? Do we listen "inwardly" in ourselves? Does such a revelation happen in the spirit's pure interiority? In a rapture and ecstasy of the soul, carried away out of the space and time of "worldliness" into the spheres beyond all appearances and images, for a speechless Thou-to-Thou of spirit to Spirit? Or is the place of God's revelation the dark interiority of a basic mood, of a feeling, in whose infinite yearning the infinite speaks? Or where else is the spot of a possible revelation of God in us? It looks as if we might still mention many other possibilities which, for a superficial glance, might [139] be considered as such a place. Every philosophy of religion is basically nothing but an attempt to say where humanity should wait for an encounter with God, where we can find our God.

But is it possible at all meaningfully to make such an attempt? Can we as it were tell God whither to come in order to meet humanity? Can we make bold to determine by ourselves the place of a possible encounter? Does such an idea not at once contradict our previous conclusions, where we said that God is supremely free, hence unpredictable for us? On the other hand, when we mention a "place" at which God's revelation must happen, is this not an *a priori* imposed by us on such a revelation? The nature of such a place for a spiritual encounter decides already by itself what can happen in it, since not everything is possible everywhere.

Even were this not the case, even if to pinpoint a spot for a possible revelation were not to determine from the start the content and manner of such a free encounter of God with humanity and thus to destroy the freedom of such a revelation, how is it possible to determine this place at all? Does not every determination mean that we stress one essential human characteristic, supposed then to be the preferred place for a revelation by God?

These considerations, submitted by way of questions, provide us already with a few insights. First, the "place" of a possible revelation of God should not be determined in such a way [140] that it restricts from the start the possibilities of such a revelation. It should not be conceived as if it might tell us *a priori* what the content of such a divine revelation may be. For in this case revelation would be but the objective counterpart of our human religious disposition. This is the basic error of every modernistic philosophy of religion, whether with the rationalists revelation is considered but another name for what the rationalistic autonomous human spirit can know about God by itself, or with Schleiermacher this disposition is conceived as the feeling of utter dependence or, in the sense of Otto, as the experience of the *mysterium tremendum et fascinosum*, or in any other way.

Each of these trends always decides, in function of a certain religious disposition and experience, "from below," in function of human nature, what may be considered the content of a possible revelation. From this vantage point it critically examines the content of a certain historical revelation and, in certain cases, some items of such a revelation are eliminated, because they do not agree with the contents of the revelation that has been set up *a priori*, or because they are not required by the latter and are thus considered unimportant.

What we have said above forces us already to reject such a conception of the place of a possible revelation. To be a human being is to be a transcendence toward being as such. It follows at once that we stand open for all being. Hence either we possess it already, and a revelation of what is always manifest is not possible, or, precisely because of this absolute transcendence, we cannot possess a previous law of what [141] can and should be revealed. To be essentially open for all being is not to be able, by oneself, to determine, by way of restriction, what may be considered as a possible object of a revelation and what not. We must stay open for all being. Since we do not yet possess all being, only the second possibility remains. On account of its unlimited transcendence, the place of a possible revelation cannot, for a spirit, contain an *a priori* law for the possibilities of what is to be revealed.

Another consequence must be considered. The manifestation of something unknown may occur in two ways: either it is presented in its own self, or some knowledge of it is mediated in word, where "word" is taken at first in the sense of a vicarious sign of what is not given in itself. Insofar as human nature is the absolute openness of the spirit for being as such, hence also for pure, absolute being, the possibilities of a revelation through the self-presentation of its object are wholly exhausted only if we were to see the absolute God immediately in God's own self.

Therefore, as long as God gives us no immediate self-manifestation, we must always take into account the possibility of a revelation of this God in the "word" (word meant in the above sense). Hence as long as we are not given the immediate vision of God, we are always and essentially, on account of our basic makeup, those who listen for God's word, those who have to reckon with a possible revelation of God that consists not in the immediate presentation in [142] God's own self as the one who is revealed, but in a communication through a vicarious sign, whereby another reality points to the one that is to be revealed.

There is a second remark to be made here about this place of a possible revelation. This place cannot, from the start, be determined in such a way that it points to a specific part of our basic makeup which would be the only chosen place for such a revelation. God can only reveal what we can hear. This statement is immediately evident. It does not imply by itself any previous limitation of the possible objects of a revelation, because of the transcendence of the human spirit toward being as such. This entails also at once that the absolute openness for being as such must be an inner moment of this place of a possible revelation. Suppose now that we modify this statement in such a way as to say: God can only reveal what we can perceive through this or that side of our nature, through this or that fundamental experience, through this or that religious feeling, through this or that

religious experience. In this case we would do away as well with
the unlimited openness of the spirit as with the free and unforeseeable nature of a possible revelation of God.

Yet the place of the possible revelation of God has not yet
been clearly determined when we say that it is our unlimited
possibility, resulting from the spirit's transcendence, to hear any
word that comes from the mouth of God. For we have not yet
adequately described our transcendence as a spirit. [143] We have
not yet grasped in its specifically *human* peculiarity. We have
said above that the only thing we can say about the place of a
possible revelation is that we ourselves are to be this place.

Thus when, in the following pages, we try to determine this
place more precisely, we are always thinking only of the peculiar nature of human transcendence, of an inner moment of it,
not of something distinct from it. Thus we must determine our
nature more completely than we have done hitherto through the
abstract statement that to be a human person is to be a finite
spirit. We must find out in what precise way the human person
is spirit. To show the purpose of these considerations, so that
their scope may become clearer, we may say: To be human is to
be spirit as a historical being [*Der Mensch is als geschichtliches Wesen
Geist*]. The place of our transcendence is always also a historical
place. Thus the place of a possible revelation is always and necessarily also our history.

General ontology has already shown us that a possible revelation must have a certain historicity. When we know God as
the pure, absolutely luminous being, God also stands before us
as one who acts freely, who has not yet exhausted the possibilities of divine freedom with respect to us by the free creation of
this finite being. But free activity is essentially historical activity. In a first, general, and metaphysical sense, there is history
wherever there is free activity, because in such an activity things
happen which cannot be deduced or computed from some general, previous ground.

[144] Such a free, undeducible happening is also always a
unique happening that cannot be repeated. It can only be understood in itself; it is not one application of some general law. Now
such an event is totally unlike an object of the natural sciences,

i.e., of a knowledge that aims at necessary and general laws that totally explain the single case. We call it a historical event, as opposed to an event in nature. Thus when we consider it from God's side, revelation is itself already seen as a historical event.

However, this brief outline of the concept of history is not yet an adequate description of what the historical is in a human history. Thus when we say: revelation is a historical event, because the place of a possible revelation for us is our history, we do not mean this in the general metaphysical sense of history as such, but in the sense of *human* history.

But what is human history? We must not merely set down a definition of it. The meaning of human history should become clear to us from an examination of our historicity in the midst of our transcendence. We must establish our historicity not merely through empirical observation, nor through the simple accumulation of concrete facts. We must understand historicity as belonging to our basic nature. As long as this had not been done, we might always imagine that, because of our spiritual nature, we might believe that we can try to put ourselves, as spirit, above our history, [145] to emancipate ourselves from it, and thus to exclude history from the start as the possible place of a revelation. As spirit we possess the absolute possibility of attempting this, not of succeeding in it. Thus we must show that turning toward our history is an inner moment of our spiritual nature. If we succeed in this, we will have also shown that the place of a possible revelation of God, namely, our openness for all being as such, is also necessarily situated within human history.

We must also inquire how it follows from the basic nature of human transcendence itself that we stand in history as spirit, that our historicity is not simply something that just happens to us among other things, but rather something which we have to be precisely *as* spirit, as open for God.

Thus we understand that such an undertaking can start only there where our transcendence itself has become visible: with the general question about being. Thus we must, in a third probe, once more analyze it, to find out what it tells us about our basic makeup. The third aspect, under which the question about being must be considered, has already been mentioned at the start of this investigation. We must inquire about being in general, in such a way that the question refers to the being of a being and thus takes into account the distinction between being and beings.

We have already said once before that the general question about being is but the most formalized way of expressing, under the guise of a question, every judgment we make, as human, necessarily and always in every thought and [146] action. Every statement says something of something: this is something of that kind. Or even more generally: this (being [*Seiende*]) has an act of being of that kind. It is easy to see that such a statement is but the formal affirmative turn of the most general question about being, under the aspect that concerns us here: what is the being of a being? Thus we must answer the following question: what follows from the analysis of this statement (whether expressed as a question or as an assertion) for the problem at hand? Insofar as this statement (in concrete form, of course) always necessarily occurs in human existence, the result of our analysis too, as implicitly affirmed with this statement, has also to be expressly affirmed.

Before we can undertake the immediate analysis of our question of being, we must remind the reader of a formerly established conclusion and we must point to a fact.

We must recall a former conclusion: Being is self-presence, as we have shown through an analysis of the general question about being. This meant, as also already mentioned, that in its first and original meaning, to know is not somehow to grasp an object, to refer intentionally to something other and foreign, but a being's self-presence, the self-reflection that belongs to a being to the extent that it possesses being, to the extent of its intensity of being. In the same connection we have also stressed the fact that being is an analogical concept, which varies intrinsically in its meaning. Therefore, a metaphysical understanding of a specific kind of being (for instance, of human being) is possible only if we start from this original metaphysical concept of knowledge [147] and take into account the inner analogous transformation of the concept of knowledge together with that of the concept of being.

We must call the attention to a fact: Human knowing is *receptive* knowing. At first we speak simply of human knowing, without distinguishing between different possible human cognitive powers. A metaphysical understanding of such different powers of knowledge cannot be reached by simply putting them together. Unity always comes before plurality. Hence the plurality of such powers should be understood in their original derivation from their unity, as the necessary unfolding of the one nature that is human nature.

About this one human knowledge we first notice the fact that it is a receptive knowledge. This means that we do not from the start, on account of our essence, possess any knowledge. This is not an obvious property belonging to all knowledge. The knowledge of the "angel," for instance, to take an example from the Thomist metaphysics of knowledge, is based upon the fact that angels are self-present by themselves, that their own natures are originally self-luminous to them, without any need of grasping something else, distinct from themselves, in order to arrive at a conscious return into themselves.

The opposite is true for us. We are present to ourselves only when we grasp another object different from ourselves, an object [148] that must come our way and show itself to us by itself. The return into oneself, the self-reflection, which constitutes the essence of knowledge, is possible to us only when we step outside ourselves toward another reality distinct from us. Anticipating what we shall explain later, we may already say that "returning into ourselves" [*Rückkehr in sich*] is for us always also "stepping out into the world" [*Auskehr in Welt*]. The former is possible only on account of the latter. When we turn toward another reality in order to know it, we do not yet have at our disposal a knowledge wholly grounded in ourselves.

Once it is admitted that human knowledge is receptive and the obvious conclusions are drawn from this fact, we see at once that we can never absolutely detach [*ablösen*] ourselves from this foreign starting point of all our knowing in such a way that it does not show up in all our knowledge. Every progress of knowledge always remains essentially tied to the first starting point. Essentially it is but the unfolding of what is originally given. If then human knowledge is essentially receptive knowledge, the basic structure of the first receptivity and of what is originally received will carry on in every subsequent knowledge and determine the structure of human knowledge as such. Human knowledge can be self-return [*Einkehr*] always only by stepping out [*Auskehr*] into the world. Hence it will be our task to determine more precisely the metaphysical structure of this starting point of receptive human knowledge. By starting point we mean not only the cognitive power in its unavoidable receptivity, [149] but also the original first object of this receptivity as such. For both of them constitute an intrinsic unity, since, on account of their original unity in being as such, knowing and being known correspond to each other. That is why every knowledge must intrinsically correspond to the object that determines it, and, more specifically in our case, receptive knowledge must correspond to what may originally be received.

It seems to us that in this way we have established what we must inquire into and whence the answer to our inquiry must come. We inquire into the place where we can meet the God of possible self-revelation. This place is our transcendence in its specifically *human* peculiarity. So we must inquire about it. The answer to the question comes again from the most general question about being. We consider it now in its third aspect. We inquire about being while keeping in mind the distinction between being and a being. In this investigation we presuppose that human knowledge is receptive. We return into ourselves by stepping outside ourselves toward an object distinct from us, which must show itself by itself to us. Hence receptive knowledge means a knowledge in which stepping out is and remains the condition of the possibility of the self-return. In the following investigations we shall have to start from such a receptive knowledge and the conditions of its possibility.

Chapter 10
The Human Person as a Material Being

Where can a possible revelation occur in the human person? This question inquires about the peculiar nature of human transcendence. We expect that this peculiarity will become apparent in the third aspect of the general question about being, which considers the basic distinction we necessarily make between being and beings. In order to go on from this starting point we found it necessary, in the last chapter, to remind the reader of something and to establish a fact. The reminder was that being is self-presence and that knowing is originally nothing but the self-presence of a being that corresponds to its intensity of being. The fact was that human knowing, hence human self-presence in a return to ourselves, is necessarily receptive, and supposes that we step outside ourselves toward something that is not ourselves and that is grasped as the first object of our knowledge.

This reminder and this fact seem to lead us into a contradiction. Knowing is supposed to be, in its innermost metaphysical essence, the knowing being's self-presence with itself. However, with such a conception of knowledge, the notion of a knowledge that is originally receptive, seems to be nonsense. True, it allows us to understand the possibility of knowing something that is distinct from the knower. Thus, when, in its self-presence, [151] a being grasps itself and knows about itself whatever may be known, it can know itself as cause and creative ground of another being. In this way it may, through its self-presence, know this other reality as a possible object of its own causality. This is the manner in which God, for instance, knows things different from God. As pure being, God grasps the divine essence and thus knows it also as the omnipotent creative ground of finite beings, and thus these beings themselves.

Our conception of knowledge starts to present difficulties for the possibility of knowing a distinct other being only when we presuppose that the latter is the *first* object of knowledge. If being means self-presence, and if knowing is nothing but the self-presence of a being, its self-reflection, then it looks as if, from the start and in principle, the first known of any knower must be the knower's *own* essence. Now the fact we have established is that human knowledge is receptive knowledge; its first object is one which stands outside, and is distinct from it; it is present to itself only by reaching out in knowledge from another and letting this object meet it; it is capable of returning into itself only by stepping out of itself into the world as distinct from itself. How can we solve this difficulty? Its solution will allow us to understand more adequately the human essence. Thus it lies wholly in the direction of our investigation.

Our question is then: How must we [152] metaphysically interpret the knowers who, in their original knowledge, are present to the *other*, if their first way of knowing has to be of this kind, although knowledge is essentially self-presence? Such a question is still possible; self-presence, being, knowing—the concepts we use in our question—are not fixed once and for all in the question itself. Otherwise the question itself would be contradictory. All of this has been shown by what we said above about the analogy of these concepts.

We answer the question first in a very formal way by stating that this being must be ontically [*seinshaft*] the being of "another." When we first start formulating this statement in a very formal way, the difficulty we try to present finds a solution. If the knower is ontically [*seinsmäßig*] a being that is present to another, it is obvious that, when it is self-present through knowledge, it is also present through knowledge to this other, to which it is ontically [*seinsmäßig*] present. If this being is the being of another, then its self-reflection is originally, and not only subsequently, the self-reflection of this other. Then what is first known in this self-reflection is the other, to which the knower is always already present as a being [*seinsmäßig*], not only through knowledge as such. The only remaining question is what this statement, which sounds so formal and so abstract, about being ontically present to another, may well mean, so that self-presence may originally and by itself be knowing presence to the other. That is what must now be explained in more detail.

Our difficulty was the seeming contradiction between our basic conception of knowledge as such and the receptivity of human knowledge. [153] We tried to solve it by saying that the being of the human being should ontically [*seinsmäßig*] be present to another, be the act of being of another. We say: being (*Sein*); we do not say: a being (*Seiendes*), because our statement referred to the luminosity of a being insofar as, and to the extent that, this being possesses being [*dieses Seiende Sein hat*] and thus to the extent that it is being. To that extent luminosity belongs to being, to the intensity of a being's being, and that is why our human being must be grasped as an ontological being-with-another.

Being, reality, actuality, as we may also put it Scholastically, does not, in us, stand in itself alone, but is with "another." It is obvious that the mysterious "other," which we have hitherto grasped only in a very formal way, cannot itself be being, intensity of being. Otherwise it would be unable to contribute a solution to our difficulty, which is: how, in human being, the self-reflection of being in itself changes into the possibility of having another reality be its first known.

Therefore this "other" must be a reality, yet no being, no known in itself, for, as such, it would reflect upon itself; it would be the ground of the knowledge of *itself*, not of the knowledge of another. This "other" is therefore the *possibility* of being which, on the one hand, is real and really distinct from being (from actuality), and on the other hand, as mere possibility, is no being, which must by itself be self-present in knowledge.

Therefore to be human is to be an empty, undetermined possibility of being, really distinct from it. That is what Thomist metaphysics calls *matter.* As shown by the way we arrived at this concept, the modern idea of a physical and chemical materiality is totally alien to it. Matter, the stuff studied by chemistry, is a thing [154] that must somehow be perceptible, at least for scientific observation. Matter in Thomist ontology is indeed a real metaphysical component of a thing, but it cannot be perceived; it should not be interpreted as a thing. Nor can we represent the real possibility of a being, really distinct from its being, as some kind of a physical basic stuff, say like the former ether of physics. It is, as it were, a postulate of metaphysics, not a postulate in the sense of the setting up of a scientific hypothesis, but in the sense of a metaphysical principle, of something that, as such, can never be the object of a scientific observation (we may observe things only, not their metaphysical principles), but that is strictly demanded for metaphysical reasons.

Human being, which the Scholastics also called form, is therefore the being of this undetermined real possibility that is called matter. Human being is self-subsisting to such an extent (we shall come back later on the reasons for this statement) that we must understand it essentially, from the very start, as the being of the other, of matter. Of its nature it subsists in another.

Let us insist once more that we have thus established an element of our basic human ontological makeup, not just one more human feature (as if it were possible to put human nature together with previously existing parts). No, we have strictly deduced this element of our essential makeup from the first starting point of human knowledge. What we have said hitherto is nothing but the Thomist principle: *The soul* [155] *is the form of the body* [*Anima humana est forma corporis*], where body is to be understood Thomistically, as prime matter [*materia prima*], as the empty real possibility of being.

Of course, this provides us only with the first and still rather vaguely understood starting point for the question with which we are expressly concerned. We will have to find out more precisely what this matter is that is postulated here as a metaphysical presupposition of human knowing. We will have to make at least somewhat clearer why this way of conceiving our human makeup as that of being in matter renders a receptive knowledge metaphysically intelligible. We will have to inquire how this starting point for our idea of the human person as a spirit develops further to make us understand the nature both of receptive knowledge itself and that of its object.

In all these endeavors we must not forget what we have already said at the beginning our investigation: on the one hand, we can speak of philosophy of religion only by constructing it from the ground up. We should not simply speak "about" it, as if we knew already before hand what it is. On the other hand, in the few pages at our disposal, we can finish this task, which coincides with metaphysics, only in the barest outline. We have to be satisfied with the hope that for the reader familiar with Thomist metaphysics we thus indicate at least how a philosophy of religion has to look within this metaphysics, whereas for the reader who does not know this metaphysics, we provide at least some idea of [156] what it contains. Nobody can expect that we should do more here.

Thus we are standing before a new starting point for our insight in the essential makeup of the human person. To be human is to be receptive knowledge in such a way that our self-knowledge, our cognitive self-subsistence derives always and necessarily from a stepping out into the world, from the grasping of something other, distinct from us, that constitutes the first object of human knowledge. Hence we concluded that a human being must be one of these beings whose being is that of an empty possibility of being distinct from itself. We must now further explain this statement.

Insofar as we derive this insight from a consideration borrowed from the metaphysics of knowledge, it is obvious that it applies to us precisely insofar as our knowledge is receptive. In other words: We are receptive knowers, and insofar as our knowledge is the reception of an object, not the *a priori* possession of some knowledge of ourselves, we are the being of matter. Now a knowledge which, as such, in its being, is the being of a possibility of being distinct from itself—real and wholly undetermined in itself, which is matter—is thus the knowledge of a material being, and is known as sense knowledge. This means that receptive knowledge in the above sense is essentially *sense* knowledge. Thus we have reached a *metaphysical* idea of human sensibility [*Sinnlichkeit*]. We have established sensibility not simply as the cognitive power which we happen to possess [157] (which would not bring us beyond an *a posteriori* description of the concrete forms of this sensibility, beyond a description that would have to start from the different sense organs). But from the metaphysically deduced essence of receptive knowledge we have concluded that this knowledge is necessarily sense knowledge. In return we have also understood the metaphysical essence of sensibility. Sensibility is the knowledge possessed by a being which, in order to have the other as its first object, must itself be the being of matter.

We must here draw attention to a methodical insight important for the whole of our metaphysics. The present instance provides a very clear example for it. We have just established a concept of matter, of subsisting-in-another, as ontological correlates
of corresponding concepts in the domain of knowledge. This
shows that, in general, really metaphysical ontological concepts
can be grasped only when combined with the corresponding
concepts of the metaphysics of knowledge. The former are but
the translation of the latter in the language of being, and the
other way round. This insight is basically but the application of
our first ontological principle about the luminosity of being. For
this principle implies that a being possesses being to the extent
that it is self-present in knowledge and the other way round.
The intensity of being [*Seinsmächtigkeit*] in its analogy, and thus
also all concepts that are connected with it and explicitate it, can
be known in their proper nature only when we consider the corresponding degree and peculiarity of self-presence in knowledge.

[158] Receptive knowledge is sense knowledge, i.e., the self-
presence of a being whose being is reality of matter [*dessen Sein
Wirklichkeit der materia ist*]. Thus we must answer the question
how this matter, in which subsists the being of one who knows
receptively through the senses, can be further elucidated. For
this would also shed light on the nature of the human person as
one who possesses such receptive sense knowledge.

In order to answer this question, we start with a prior question: What must be the metaphysical structure of the being which
is the first known *object* of a receptive knowledge? If knowing is
originally self-presence of being, we may also say: the ontological structure of the knower is the *a priori* law of its possible objects as such. The structure of a being that has a certain intensity
of being may be translated into the structure of a self-presence,
therefore into that of its *first* known object as such. For if being
is self-presence and if knowing is self-presence of being, then
the first known is always the knower's own being itself, so that
the structure of a knower as a being is the structure of the known
and the other way round. And when what is first known is the
other, and when this is so because the being that knows becomes
being of the other, we reach again the same conclusion: the structure of the knower as a being is the structure of the known. This

implies that, if the being of the receptive sense knower is the being of matter, the known itself must be material in this sense.

Thus we may say: the original object of receptive knowledge can only be the being that is rooted in matter [159] as its reality. The object of sensibility, of human receptive knowledge, is the material being. Thus the insight into the nature of material things as the first, original objects of human receptive knowledge provides us, in turn, with the possibility of explaining more precisely our notion of matter and thus of interpreting better the essence of the human person as material being.

We may now return explicitly to the third aspect of our general question about being. We grasp being always as the being of a being. We always grasp an existing reality, a real whatness of this or that determined kind as that of a "subject." As shown in the most general and formal way, precisely in this manner of formulating our question about being, we distinguish in every object of our knowledge between a *what* in a something, and this *something* itself, as determined by this whatness, between a form and a subject, between an essence and that which possesses it [*Träger*]. An object is represented in our knowledge always only in the peculiar way of such a distinction.

The subject, to which the whatness is attributed as its substantial determination and to which the whatness known and expressed in the concept is referred, in other words, the "wherein" of a whatness and the "whereunto" of our attribution of it, cannot itself in its turn be an act of being. For, as such, it would be an existing reality, that can be grasped, that is self-luminous. Hence it might be expressed itself as a whatness and it should itself, in its turn, be [160] referred to another subject.

Therefore this "wherein" of an existing reality and "whereunto" to which in knowledge we refer a conceptually grasped whatness can only be the empty undetermined possibility of being. Thus we stand once more before matter, this time by considering the peculiar way in which we grasp a being, and we arrive at similar conclusions. However, the present approach may help us better explain what matter is. We saw it as the empty, undetermined "wherein" of an existing reality which we grasp conceptually and attribute through a judgment precisely to this matter. Now in the judgment, in which it is present as the content of the predicate, this whatness always comes up as general whereas matter (as the whereunto to which the predicate is referred) is seen as the undetermined bearer, that can of itself be the indifferent subject of several possible whatnesses. Because the whatness is general, matter appears as the ground which, on account of its emptiness and its indifference for any determined whatness, makes it possible for this multipliable whatness to be this or that well determined whatness. As the whereunto of the statement and the underlying wherein of the whatness itself, matter is thus the cause of the "thisness" of a being, whose whatness may be reproduced. In this sense matter is the principle of individuation. Not, of course, in the sense of an individuality which, through its peculiar fullness, would be in the unique nature of its determinations, the opposite of something that may be reproduced. But in the sense of an individuality belonging to a being whose several quidditative determinations, even when combined in possibly the most complex [161] way, may, in principle, still always be repeated.

Hence matter is the principle of individuation, not in the sense that it is the cause of the unicity of a certain quiddity, but in the sense that is the cause of the multiple individuation of the same quiddity. From this explanation of matter, we may now derive further information both about human nature and about the nature of the object to be received by our receptive knowledge. We shall speak of this in the following chapter.

At any rate, we have reached the following conclusion: Human beings are spirits in such a way that, in order to become spirit, we enter and we have ontically [*seinshaft*] always already entered into otherness, into matter, and so into the world. This is not simply another statement about human nature to be added to the assertion of our spiritual nature. It is an inner determination of our spirituality itself. This should not be understood as if spirituality [*Geistigkeit*], as a *peculiar* power of human beings, were sensible. Such a statement would contain an inner contradiction. It is meant in the sense that we are spirit in a peculiar way. Our human spirit is *receptive*—*anima tabula rasa*—and because of its receptivity this spirit needs, as its own, indispensable means, produced by itself, a sense power through which it may strive toward its own goal, the grasping of being as such. In this sense to be human is to be sense-endowed spirituality [*sinnliche Geistigkeit*]. The intellectual soul [*anima intellectiva*], i.e., the spirit, really and essentially informs the body [*est vere et essentialiter corpus informans*], to use the words of the Council of Vienna. The soul as spirit enters by itself, *per se*, into matter. We have also already discovered a starting point to help us understand matter better. Matter is the principle [162] of individuation. We shall now further have to inquire what it means for the spirit that we human persons wend our way through the world precisely as spirit.

Chapter 11
The Human Person as a Historical Spirit

The soul, form of matter [*Anima forma materiae*]. This was the statement the last chapter started to establish. At the same time we had discovered a starting point that helped us understand prime matter. It is the empty, undetermined, although real possibility of being and, as such, the ground of the multiple individuation of the same quiddity. We have also already said that such an explanation of the nature of a material being told us something about ourselves as endowed with receptive knowledge and about the first objects of this knowledge, which have to show themselves in order to be known. The empty potential indetermination of matter as real and by itself pure possibility, allows us to state two more things about it: It is the ground of the *spatiality* and of the *temporality* of the being of which it is an essential component.

It is the ground of the spatiality of a being. The quiddity, the object of our knowledge, appeared to us as by itself universal, indifferent to be a particular this or that, hence as a determination that can come to stand as often as one pleases in the wherein of the matter [163] that bears it. When such a form, such a quiddity, does in fact repeatedly subsist in matter, so that the same reality is several times repeated, it becomes possible to add up these several reproductions. Counting is possible only where what is to be counted appears previous to the counting, as the repetition of the same. And since matter is the principle of the possible repetition of the same, we must necessarily consider it as the principle of number. But number implies quantity. Matter is the principle of quantity, since the latter is but the multiple repetition of the same.

Now matter is such a principle not only with respect to several things that are really distinct from each other; it must also carry out this, its essential function, within the single thing into which it enters as an essential principle. Hence it makes of the

single thing something quantitative *in itself*. Now the repetition
of the same within one and the same thing is nothing but its
spatiality, its being intrinsically affected by quantity, the real diversity of the same thing within its unity. Thus we may say: a
being whose innermost makeup [*Seinskonstitution*] contains matter as an inner essential principle is spatial.

The further basic determination of a material object is its
inner temporality. We saw that matter appears the in itself undetermined possibility of real determinations. This implies that
it is always wider than the determined reality whose substratum
[*Träger*] it is in this or that determined being. The determined
quiddity, which subsists in matter, [164] does not fill matter's whole
potentiality. Thus, because of the ever wider range and incom-
pleteness of its matter, a material being always points toward
new determination; it is always "in motion" toward new realities
of being that always open up in the ground of its nature, because
of the undetermined range of the possibilities of matter.

Hence the material being is one that always points toward
the totality of the realization of its possibilities as the future of its
inner movement and keeps striving toward it. Since these possible determinations, whose simultaneous realization would constitute the realization of matter's unlimited potentialities, exclude
each other at least partially as simultaneous determinations of
the underlying matter, the totality of the possible realizations of
the potentiality of matter is always delayed and is never given all
at once.

The total realization of the possibilities of a material being is
possible only in the succession of the latter's intrinsic movement.
In other words: the being is temporal. Temporality is meant here
in the original sense, not as the extrinsic measure of the thing,
but as the inner protracting of the thing itself in the realized
totality of its possibilities. As realized, these possibilities cannot
at once determine this being. Because it is material, each one of
them is perishable and dynamically finalized toward another
possibility that will overtake it. Thus we must say that a material
being is intrinsically temporal. In this way we have established
three determinations of matter: It explains how the same may be
repeated over and over again. It provides the being [165] of which

it is an essential constituent with an inner spatiality and temporality.

We have seen that to be a human knower, whose knowledge
is essentially receptive, is thus to a being in matter. On account
of the intrinsic nature of our knowledge, our being is that of
matter. In this sense, we are material beings. We must now use
this deeper insight into the nature of matter to reach a metaphysical concept of human nature.

To be human is to be one among many. We are essentially in
space and in time. Insofar as our quiddity is, by itself, the quiddity of matter, it is a reality that may, in principle, be identically
reproduced. An individual human is, in principle, one of a kind.
Of course, no attempt is made here to deduce *a priori* in a metaphysical deduction, the fact of a biological bond through reproduction or the concrete manner of such a biological connection.
This is the task of empirical observation of facts. But something
may be known *a priori* and through metaphysical insight: that,
because we are essentially material beings, we may be repeated
in our quiddity, in our nature, that there may exist many human
beings.

This implies also that, should there in fact exist only one
human person, that one would by nature have to carry an ordination to a possible multiplicity of other human person. When
we spoke of the temporality of a material thing, we had already
stressed the fact that a single material being can never wholly
and at once realize the ever greater range of its possibilities that
always are already contained in its materiality. It follows that a
single human person can never exhaustively, and at one time,
actualize all that belongs to it by way of possibilities [166] as a
material being. That is why referring to other beings of one's
own kind, which everyone does as this particular individual, is
not something unimportant; it is a referring to a multitude of
human beings, to a humanity which, only as a whole, can really
make manifest that which is essentially given to each of us single
persons deep down in our possibilities, but only as possibilities.
We are actually human only in a humanity.

Everyone knows what we mean by saying that as material
beings we are spatial and temporal. We are not put into a spa-

tiotemporal world after having first been made into human beings. We are not simply put on a spatiotemporal stage to set out our lives. Spatiotemporality is our inner makeup, and belongs properly to us as human. Because matter is one of our essential components, we ourselves construct space and time as intrinsic components of our existence.

When we say: To be a human person is essentially to be one among many of our kind, with whom we are together in space and time on account of our inner essence, we say nothing but: We are historical, in the concrete sense of a *human* history. Above we have already, in a true and necessary although wider sense, attributed a historicity to human activity. We are historical insofar as we are the ones who act [167] freely, even in our transcendence toward God, hence in determining our relation to the absolute. Of course, this moment belongs essentially to human historicity. There is authentic historicity only where there is the uniqueness and the unforeseeability of freedom. Although nature changes and undergoes movement, it has no real history, because all stages of its movement, although their direction may be irreversible, are but necessary moments and consequences of the initial setup and therefore instances of a general law. There is history only where singularity and originality triumph over being only an instance or an item in a series. There is history only where there is freedom.

But there is history in the *human* sense only where, in a togetherness of free persons [*zusammen freien Personen*] in their multiplicity, the activity of freedom expands in a world, i.e., in space and time, where the intelligible acts of freedom must, in order to become manifest, extend in space and time, where they need space-time in order to be themselves.

And precisely such a historicity is found in us because we are essentially free, self-subsisting personalities [*insichselber-ständigen Persönlichkeiten*] who must freely realize ourselves through a multiplicity of such personalities as the total realization of the very essence of such a personality in space and time.

A human being is a historical being. This is now for us no longer a mere observation resulting from the accumulation of disparate facts, which are then afterwards put together. It is an essential insight, whose elements we understand as they derive from their original starting point in their [168] necessary and inner connection.

Before we put these data in immediate relation with our problem in the philosophy of religion, we must add a few more remarks to the above considerations. The first one concerns the relation between our investigations and the principles of Thomist ontology. Anyone familiar with the latter will have no trouble admitting that our deductions agree with this ontology.

We started from the fact that human knowledge is receptive. This is a basic view of the Thomist metaphysics of knowledge which it shares with Aristotle: *Anima tabula rasa*. All our ideas derive from a contact with the world of sense. Thomas not only rejects inborn ideas, but also another kind of objective apriorism in knowledge, namely, the intuition of the ideas in the Augustinian sense. For even such an intuition would provide for us an objective knowledge that would originally be independent of our sense knowledge and would operate as a norm of the world of sense perception only after the latter had been constituted.

From the receptive character of our human knowledge we have, in a transcendental deduction, arrived at the concepts of sense knowledge and of matter. It is true that Thomas knows of other ways that lead to the knowledge of matter; but he knows also of this one. He speaks explicitly of a *via praedicationis* (*In VII Metaph.*, lect. 2, no. 1287), in which human beings reach a knowledge of matter.

We might also show that for Thomas receptive knowledge and [169] sense knowledge are essentially the same thing. This proof might be conducted in different ways. It might, for instance, be undertaken by starting from the Thomist metaphysics of angelic knowledge. If our thesis is correct, the angels, as immaterial beings, cannot possess any receptive knowledge. Thus we might show that, for these reasons, Thomas must hold that the knowledge angels have of things distinct from them must be conceived not as a receptive knowledge (i.e., as one that gets its content from the things themselves), but as a knowledge brought about through inborn ideas and through a sharing of God's active knowledge, hence as a *scientia quasi activa*.

Another way of establishing the same thesis would consist in showing that for Thomas a real ontic action of one being upon another, and that is presupposed by all receptive knowledge in this world, is possible only among material beings. However, these short hints will have to do here. (See *Spirit in the World*, passim).

If we understand the materiality of the human being in this way, as one which receives its knowledge from the things themselves, the further determinations of such a material being in a Thomist ontology makes no more difficulties. As we saw above, matter is for Thomas the principle of individuation, the principle of quantity and of movement, and so finally, of time, properly speaking (in contrast with a "historicity" as it exists in the *aevum* of the angels, or, in a certain sense, in the absolutely extra-temporal activity of God's freedom). Thus the method and the conclusions [170] of this part of our metaphysical anthropology are definitely Thomist.

The second remark refers to the following question: Why does the materiality of the knowing subject metaphysically explain the possibility of receptive knowledge of an object distinct from the knower? For it is perhaps not yet totally clear what the presence of a merely undetermined real possibility in the knower may contribute here. One might object that our deduction of the materiality of a receptive knowledge, through the dialectical juggling with the concept of receptive knowledge and with the principle of the self-presence of being, leads only to a verbal agreement between these two presuppositions.

In the premises the "other" that is supposed to be the first known object of receptive knowledge is the object which is really distinct from the knower. This is the object that receptive cognition knows. On the other hand, in the conclusion of our deduction, the "other" to which the knower is ontically present is the empty possibility of matter, hence an intrinsic component of the knower's own being. Thus one might think that we have invalidly put two totally different things under the mere word, "the other," to which the knower is supposed to be present both as being and as knower.

It is true that the other which is known is a determination of an object distinct from the knower, while the other to which the

knower is ontically present, in which we are supposed to subsist, is prime matter. Yet our deduction is correct. This might be
shown in different ways. We chose [171] the simplest, although it
may not be the one which derives from the innermost nature of
the thing itself.

We start from the Scholastic axiom *Motus est actus moventis*
[Movement is an act of the mover] and *Motus est in moto* [The
movement is in that which is moved]. The action of a being upon
another, that follows upon the substantial makeup of both, is a
reality of the acting thing itself, hence a determination that belongs properly to it. Yet, as such, it can exist only in the being
that is influenced. Let us apply this to the ontic determination
which the sense object confers upon a subject endowed with sense
knowledge.

The influence is the reality of the sense object itself (the movement is an act of the mover), yet it unfolds, as it were, necessarily within the subject endowed with sense knowledge; hence it is
at the same time a reality of the sense knower, its determination,
and the determination of the known object that shows itself
through its activity. This reality is known in the knower because
it is the knower's determination; at the same time, it is grasped
as the determination of the sense object itself. But if a determination is to be thus, as in a neutral zone, at the same time the
reality of what moves and of what is moved, in our case, of what
knows and what causes the knowledge, this presupposes the
materiality of both.

This is obvious in Thomist ontology. Movement in the proper
sense is conceivable only in a material being. But it is also easy
to understand. The demonstration of this necessity runs along
the line of our former demonstration of the necessity of materiality in receptive [172] knowledge.

The neutral point, this common sphere, in which the determination of one may be that of the other being, is precisely the
undetermined, empty, yet real possibility which, as such, exists
in all material beings not as multiple and repeated, but as the
same empty quantitative unity in pure multiplicity. It manifests
itself in space. Space likewise is not something that might be
multiplied, nor does it possess a unity that excludes an unlimited
plurality of its parts. Matter is one and many in the domain of

substantial principles, as space is in what can be known through
the senses. There are not many "spaces," for all are but parts of
the one space; yet there is not one space that might uphold its
unity against an unrestricted plurality. The same is true for matter, which is precisely the principle of the intrinsic spatiality of a
being. It is not "many" in the many things, as if it might be repeated many times over as the same in the single things. Yet it is
not one in the sense that it would by itself exclude a sundering in
the multiplicity of the many things.

That is precisely why it can be the medium, the otherness as
such, in which what moves and what is moved share, as it were,
a determination that belongs to both. For every spatiality, in
which action stands as a determination of the agent, is likewise
the spatiality of that which undergoes the action, because it is
the manifestation of matter, which is one in the sense described
above. The otherness that two beings share, as it were, by being
rooted in the same matter, is the condition that makes it possible
that a reality of the one may also be that of the other. Without
this common medium [173] of a empty "otherness" which as such
is one, it would not be possible for a certain quidditative reality
to be one which belongs at the same time to the agent and to that
which undergoes the action. As some reality (form, act) steps
out of itself and becomes the determination of another that lacks
all determination, i.e., of matter, the ontic reality of another being, rooted in this matter, becomes *ipso facto* its own ontic reality.
And if we grasp the latter, we receptively get to know the reality
of the other.

In fine, only where there is matter can the movement be at
the same time the act of what moves [*movens*: a mover] and of
what is moved. That is why it is only in the domain of matter
that receptive knowledge is possible; here a reality is that of the
agent, which moves, yet it may be known by itself because it is
at the same time also the reality of the knower as moved by the
object of knowledge.

After these complementary remarks we return to our theme.
As our metaphysical anthropology has developed, we have come
to know the human person as a spirit in history. We are essentially beings subsisting in matter. Matter is the ground of multi-

plication of the same, of the spatiotemporality of a being. Thus we are essentially human in humankind; in space and time we carry out the work of our freedom together with the whole of humankind. We live as historical beings.

We have undertaken this analysis of human historicity with a view to a philosophy of religion. [174] We wished to know where for humanity is the place of a possible revelation of the free God, since we had discovered that we are the beings who, on account of our transcendence, stand in free love before the free God of a possible revelation. From the start of our question about the place of a possible revelation, we have said that the absolute transcendence toward being as such must be an inner moment of this place of a possible revelation. Otherwise the place of such a revelation itself would already constitute for its content a restricting *a priori* law. This would go against the authentic notion of a revelation. We said further that such a revelation must be expected as, at least possibly, coming through the word.

Finally we have already shown that, if we wished to establish the place of a possible revelation more precisely than through the absolute transcendence of the human spirit and through the word, this might only be done by making clearer the human peculiarities of this transcendence and thus the peculiar nature of the word of God as perceptible to our human nature. It could not be done by making of one specific aspect of our basic makeup the privileged place of the process of revelation.

With this in mind we undertook to develop a more explicit idea of human nature. We discovered, to put it briefly, our historicity. But this has not yet brought us to the end of our task. The question arises, what this historicity has to do with the transcendence. For, strictly speaking, we were not looking for a peculiarity of human nature, [175] but of our absolute transcendence.

But it has not yet become clear why and to what extent our historicity determines our openness for a God of a possible free revelation and makes of it a human obediential potency for a revelation, and how this openness differs from the openness for revelation that might exist in another possible finite spirit. Only when this has been explained shall we have established the great lines of the obediential potency for a revelation, as it derives from an ontology of the human person. For this purpose we must first explain the essential relations between transcendence and historicity insofar as this can be done in a metaphysical anthropology. Next we must find out what follows thence for the immediate purpose of a philosophy of religion. Thus we have briefly outlined our next tasks.

Chapter 12
Spirit and Historicity: Being and Appearance

If we wish to show the connection between the transcendence of the human spirit and human historicity, we must once more explain how we arrived at this historicity of the human person. We have not simply established it as a fact, but we have transcendentally deduced it from a peculiarity of the human spirit [176] as such. For we started from the fact that, despite its transcendence toward being as such, the human spirit is receptive knowledge.

As human we do not view the unlimited domain of all being as such in such a way that we anticipate this knowledge by starting from a certain fund of knowledge that would be available to us *a priori* together with our nature. Human openness for being as such does not derive from a previous, albeit narrower openness, which would come to us with our very nature, making known to us some objects, such as our essence itself. Rather transcendence opens up for us when we receive an object given from without, showing itself by itself. This peculiarity of our spiritual nature and transcendence was the starting point whence we arrived at human historicity. This implies that historicity is not a property that belongs *also* to us, who happen besides also to be a spirit. Rather it is an essential element of the transcendental spirituality itself. Historicity derived from the specifically human spirituality. Hence it is the historicity of the human spirit as such. We must now examine what this means.

We have said that we have our transcendence, our outlook on being as such, only because and in as much is we are receptive knowledge. Now we have also shown that receptive knowledge is intrinsically sense knowledge. Hence we know of being as such only because and insofar as we know through the senses.

[177] We must not understand this statement as if we had some sense knowledge and, subsequently, as a spirit, would, as it were, try to find out what we can do with it and the objects it offers to us. We have seen that sense knowledge, with its sen-

sible and material characteristics, is a necessary condition of that transcendence toward being as such, that possesses its openness only because a single object manifests itself to it by itself. This implies that human sensibility is correctly interpreted only when we understand it as deriving from the spirit and its necessity. This spirit which, by itself and despite its transcendence, is *tabula rasa*, can reach the fullness of its nature only if it produces a sensibility as its own power. A spirit of this kind penetrates into matter in order to become spirit. We penetrate into the world in order to reach being as such, which extends beyond the world.

Such a conception of human sensibility corresponds fully to Thomas's metaphysics of knowledge (see *Spirit in the World*, pp. 246 ff.), which explicitly conceives sensibility as a power emerging from the spirit, as the latter reaches for [*Hingreifen*] and projects toward [*Vorsprung*] the end belonging to it as spirit: to be openness for being as such.

Human sensibility is not to be understood as a power existing mainly for itself, but from the start as a power of the spirit for its own purpose. It follows that the spirit possesses its openness, its stance before being as such, hence also before pure being, only because and insofar as, [178] through its entrance into matter, it acquires an openness for, a stance before the material things in space and time.

Hence for us as finite and receptive spirits there exists a luminosity of being as such only in the luminosity of material realities; we turn toward being as such only when turning to material being; we go out toward God [*Ausgang zu Gott*] only by entering into the world [*Eingang in die Welt*]. And insofar as the access to God is given to us only in our *a priori* structure as spirit, only in the transcendence belonging properly to us, hence in our return into ourselves, we may also say: only by stepping out [*Auskehr*] into the world can we so enter into [*Einkehr*] ourselves that we encounter being and God.

When, in this connection, we speak of material things, this concept should not be restricted to the entities which, on account of their sense qualities, are immediate objects of our external senses. This concept comprises all that can immediately be given to a receptive knowledge that grasps a single object. Thus we are not thinking only of outside sense objects, but also

of ourselves, insofar as we grasp ourselves in our concrete singularity while knowing such objects and dealing with them. We
may designate all this in one word as the "world."

Insofar as all these things, which constitute the world, are
objects of a receptive knowledge, they must show themselves by
themselves. They must and can appear by themselves in their
own nature. So we may designate all this as "appearance" [*Er-
scheinung*], without in the least implying [179] that what is thus
receptively known only "seems" to be real. The word only wishes
to convey the idea that these objects "appear" in their own selves
and are not simply known on the basis of a knowledge of something else which shows itself; further, that in these immediate
objects of the receptive knowledge of a spirit, being as such is
given by the *Vorgriff*, in such a way that it "appears" in them and
only in them. In receptive knowledge the world appears in its
own self, and it causes being, which is always more than the
being of the world, to appear in the self of the world, so far as
this is possible for the finite human spirit on account of its receptive nature.

Thus we may formulate the question which concerns us here
as follows: we must investigate more thoroughly the relation ob-
taining in the spirit's transcendence between appearance and
openness of being as such.

We must first remember what we have said above about transcendence itself. We said that a human being does not stand in
an environment [*Umwelt*] as a passive part of it, but as self-subsisting before a world of objects. Through our judgment and
activity, we extrapose these objects as things in their own selves.
This allows us to return into ourselves, to be self-subsistent in
knowledge. In this self-subsistence we grasp the objects under
concepts, under a universal point of view. This comes out in every statement, since such a statement always attributes to a subject a universal quiddity (the predicate).

We have shown above how the *Vorgriff* toward being as such
is the [180] transcendental condition of the possibility for this self-
subsistence and this grasping of the things under universal concepts. By *Vorgriff* we meant the *a priori* power, given with the
very nature of the spirit, to represent to oneself the single quid-
dities brought up by the receptive sense knowledge in a dynamic

a priori reaching out of the spirit for the absolute range of its possible objects. The single object is grasped as a stage in the reaching out of the spirit for the complete fulfillment of its capacity. Thus from the start an object is always already seen under the horizon of the last end of the spirit as such.

The *Vorgriff* is the transcendence of the spirit, the surpassing of the spirit, in which we grasp the single object because, in a certain sense, we already look beyond it into the absolute range of our possible objects as such. We have also shown that this transcendence is not simply a transcendence toward a finite circle of possible objects, nor originally a transcendence toward nothingness, but that it is a transcendence toward pure being that has no intrinsic limits in itself.

It is evident that we should not understand this *Vorgriff* as an inborn idea of being as such, and even less as an objective intuition of some separate idea of being or of God's pure being itself. For all this would stand in contradiction with the statement that human knowledge is originally receptive. Should we think of the *Vorgriff* in one of the above mentioned ways, humanity would be in possession of a knowledge that is absolutely independent of receptive sense knowledge of [181] single objects in the world, hence absolutely independent of what appears. Hence the *Vorgriff* as such is not an *a priori* knowledge of an object, but the manner, given with our very nature and in that sense *a priori*, in which we take up a sense object given *a posteriori*, the *a priori* way of knowing what appears *a posteriori*. It is not a self-subsisting grasp of being as such, but the anticipation [*Vorgriff*] of being, which is possible only in grasping the appearance.

This enables us to determine more precisely the relation between transcendence and appearance. We may distinguish three moments in an appearance:

1) The appearance insofar as it is given to us only by receptive sense knowledge as such. Hence the sense object insofar as, through its own operation, it imprints itself by itself into our material sense receptivity and that makes an appearance;

2) the outlook upon being as such opened up in the *Vorgriff*. Because sensibility is a power that the spirit begets in order to reach its own end, the single sense object is from the start grasped by human knowledge in the dynamic striving of the spirit to-

ward being as such. Hence when we understand the sense object the *Vorgriff* itself enters into action; the *Vorgriff* becomes conscious and thus, through its own limitless range, it opens up for the spirit the unlimited range of being as such. When we understand the appearances, being itself is by anticipation understood in its wider range.

3) The appearance insofar as it is grasped itself under the *Vorgriff* toward being as such. We must not imagine the process as if the appearance were given to [182] human consciousness in its mere sense givenness, and as if, besides it, there would open up an outlook upon the domain of being as such. We have established the *Vorgriff* in a transcendental deduction only as the condition of the possibility of understanding the appearance in the specifically *human* way, i.e., under universal concepts and in the self-subsistence of the knower.

In other words: The sense object is, as it were, informed by the *Vorgriff*, and by the knowledge of being as such provided by it. A synthesis is made of the mere material appearance and the knowledge opened up in the *Vorgriff* of being as such. The appearance is comprehended as being, *sub ratione entis*, and only because the appearance is comprehended as a being do we acquire a knowledge of being as such. Hence we have three elements: [1] the sense appearance as such, [2] the knowledge of being (*Sein*), [3] the being (*Seiende*) as the synthesis of sense appearance and knowledge of being as such. The two first elements, if we may call them that, appear first in immediate knowledge always only as synthesized in the being that is known. Were this not the case, sense knowledge and *Vorgriff* would represent two powers in us each of which would by itself alone and independently of the other comprehend an object. But this is impossible both for the *Vorgriff*, because of the receptive character of human knowledge, and for sense knowledge, because we have seen that the spirit causes it to emanate from itself as its own power.

Thus, looking backwards, we understand better why we said that the third aspect [183] of our general question of being is that the being is comprehended as the being of a being, whereby we both separate and connect being and a being, and we refer being to a subject distinct from it and whose being it is. This is but another way of saying that through the *Vorgriff* we comprehend being only through the concept of a certain single being given through the senses. Being and a being are not the same things, for pure being is the ultimate whither of the spirit in its absolute transcendence. Here it can no longer be analyzed into being and a subject which only shares being. But what being is becomes clear to our finite receptive knowledge only in the reception of a sense object that is comprehended as a stage of the spirit on its way to being as such. That is why it is comprehended as a participation of being as such, as in possession of being to the extent of its essence.

The *Vorgriff* and that which is manifested by it are known only insofar as the *Vorgriff* is the form of the appearance, and constitutes the horizon under which the appearance is seen. Yet precisely as such it stands revealed as reaching beyond the circle of possible appearances. We have shown that its absolutely unlimited range is what allows it to make of the sense appearance an *object* opposed to human self-subsistence.

We have already pointed out above that ontological concepts are but the ontological version of concepts belonging to the metaphysics of knowledge. This is rather obvious if we remember the basic relation which makes of being and knowing an ultimate unity. Once more we notice [184] this here: The relation of knowing to appearance corresponds, on the level of knowledge, to the ontic unity of form and matter. The fact that spiritual knowledge essentially reaches beyond the circle of the appearance, while turning toward it, corresponds to the ontic self-subsistence of the same principle of being (the form) which is the reality of matter. The form subsists in itself and stands in matter, one through and in the other, exactly as the *Vorgriff* reaches beyond the world toward being as such, yet reaches being only by grasping the appearance, the world.

If we wish to set down in a few statements these briefly outlined relations between transcendence and appearances, we may put it as follows:

1) Being as such opens up for human nature *only in the appearance*. This has become quite evident first for the knowledge that refers immediately to the objects of sense experience. Their objectivity as opposed to the self-subsistence of the human subject depends on the *Vorgriff*. To that extent we know already of

being as such in our knowledge of and dealing with the things of our world. We know of it insofar and only insofar as such a knowledge is a previous condition, the horizon for the objective conceptual knowledge of the material objects we perceive. They are the first starting point, hence also the lasting foundation of all our knowledge. This explains why, even in our transcendental reflection [185] upon the conditions of our immediate objective knowledge we ever remain dependent on this starting point. In such reflection the object of knowledge changes, but not its structure, hence neither the way in which we must grasp the objects upon which the *Vorgriff* makes an outlook possible.

Even when we objectively represent being insofar as it is *not* restricted to the world as the possible totality of appearances, hence being, whose knowledge through the *Vorgriff* was the condition of the objective knowledge of the appearances, this being too must be represented after the manner of an object of the world, of an appearance. Even pure being and all immaterial realities are represented by us after the matter of material things, i.e., as a subject (as matter) to which belongs a universal quiddity, as a being that possesses being. We are utterly unable to represent in any other way that which is self-subsisting, that which exists in itself.

This shows us, precisely when we try to think of pure being and in general of immaterial realities, that all our concepts unavoidably derive from receptive sense knowledge. In Thomist terminology our first statement is, "The soul knows nothing without a phantasm" [*Nihil sine phantasmata intelligit anima*]. Even when we must grasp something that, according to its own nature, cannot be a spatiotemporal appearance, because it is not material and thus cannot show itself in itself to some receptive knowledge, even then we cannot know it without turning to an appearance in which what cannot appear takes on an appearance in a way we still have to explain. Thus in both direct and [186] reflective metaphysical knowledge, being can be comprehended only in a phenomenon.

2) The *whole of being* is opened for us in what appears. The whole of being cannot appear in itself to a receptive knowledge. Such a knowledge is essentially sense knowledge, hence it requires a material sense object to determine it. But such an object

is in space and time. Hence what is not in space and time cannot, as such, in itself, appear to a receptive knowledge. Yet being as such may be opened for receptive knowledge in an appearance. In our analysis of the human person as a spirit we have already shown that, in the *Vorgriff*, as it passes beyond the appearance, being as such opens up for us as what enables us to grasp the appearance as an object. Thus in the *Vorgriff* at least the most general structure of being as such, i.e., everything which belongs to being as being, is co-known [*mitgewußt*] by us.

These most general structures, which belong to being as such, are called the transcendental determinations of being. We have already briefly established them. Being is self-presence, self-luminosity, self-affirmation, will and value. Hence at least in this general way, being as such is made known to us in the appearance, insofar, namely, as these most general determinations of being are known. We might of course say more about them than we do here.

But the question comes up: Is it possible for knowledge that possesses the above characteristics of a receptive knowledge, for the knowledge of the human spirit, to know a *determined* being, that cannot appear in itself, that stands outside [187] the world? In other words: Can we through the intramundane [*innerweltlich*] appearance come to know extramundane [*ausserweltlich*] being only in its most general, undifferentiated structures, or also in its own proper nature, in its own specific features?

We do already know one extramundane being—God—in a concept that belongs to God and only to God. We have determined God's essence as that of pure, absolute, limitless being. This concept can, of its very essence, belong only to one being, namely, to the one we call God. But when we remember how we reached the necessity of affirming a divine being, it is easy to see that we have, in this way, come to know God only within a general doctrine of being and a metaphysics of knowledge as the objective condition of the possibility of a finite being and of its affirmation.

Hence we know of God only in function of the world and of its own existence. To speak with Thomas, God is not the "topic" [*subjectum*] of a special science that might directly inquire about

God, but is only the "principle of the topic" [*pricipium subjecti*] of a science, namely, of general ontology.

Our question then is the following: God, the immaterial and extramundane being, appears always necessarily in the appearance, because of its necessary dependence on God. Can God also further show through the appearance in such peculiarities of divine being and activity [188] that have not yet always and necessarily shown themselves in the appearance?

It is only when this question is answered that our investigation reaches its end. We are asking about the place of a possible revelation of God in humanity. Hitherto we have answered: In human transcendence, which, as such, is historicity. Or, from the objective point of view, in the appearance in the world, which manifests being as such. But not everything has thus been said. For the question is whether the appearance provides and can provide only a vague glance upon the general structures of the supramundane act of being and also of other beings of this kind. Or can these beings possibly also be known in their determinations through and in the appearance?

We must, of course, not understand this question as if we presupposed that we might, by ourselves, beyond the general structures of being as such, come to know supramundane beings in their concrete determinations. Since the *Vorgriff* by itself alone reveals what lies beyond the appearances only to the extent required for the objective knowledge of the appearance itself and for conscious human self-subsistence in the world, such a thing is *a priori* impossible. The *Vorgriff* suffices for knowledge of the most general structures of being.

Hence we are not speaking here of our possibility of knowing through the appearance solely in function of ourselves a supramundane being in its concrete specific features. But we must inquire whether a supramundane being might be made known in its concrete nature by God, whether the appearance, beyond its [189] function of manifesting being as such, which belongs necessarily to it, might be used by a supramundane being itself for a further manifestation of the latter's own nature, or whether such a manifestation is possible only if the appearance is bypassed and eliminated, hence outside of the normal procedure of human knowledge.

It is only if we can answer this question in the sense of the former possibility that it becomes evident that humanity may and must expect a revelation of God within *that* domain in which we are always already standing: the domain of transcendence which is also always already historicity. This is the question we must answer. This answer constitutes at the same time (after the two above statements) the third statement in which we try to formulate the relation between transcendence and appearance.

Chapter 13
The Human Historicity of a Possible Revelation

As spirit we are destined for being as such. We possess this transcendence only in connection with the spatiotemporal appearance in which we ourselves belong, hence in connection with historical appearance. But when we grasp it, we stand open for all being. Is this true only in the sense of a knowledge of the transcendental characteristics of being as such? Or can a specific [190] supramundane being be made known through the appearance? And in what way is this conceivable? This is the question which we must now consider.

We reply with a statement, which is at the same time the third one among the statements in which we tried to formulate the relation between our transcendence and immanence in the world. This third statement is: Every being can be made manifest in the appearance *through the word*. This statement, the most important one for our further considerations on the philosophy of religion, needs a more thorough explanation.

First we must keep in mind two things we know already: The *Vorgriff* opens up the horizon for absolutely all being. Hence we know already about positive determinations of absolutely every being. On the other hand not every being can in itself be present to receptive knowledge. How then can such a being be known nonetheless in its specific nature?

We answer first: through negation. In order really to understand this manner of knowing something that is not presented in itself, we must first come back to the analogy of being. A being may not be conceived as a sum of sundry properties, each of which, shut up as it were within itself, stands besides the others in mere juxtaposition. Rather, what we call the properties of a being are nothing but the expression of the degree of intensity of being that something possesses. Now this intensity of being may be negatively determined by negation. In this way we may also reach a certain being outside of the realm of appearance.

Through the *Vorgriff* [191], in the analogy of our concept of being, we reach from the start, although in an empty way, all possible degrees of the intensity of being, from the pure possibility of prime matter up to pure being. On the other hand, in the appearances, specified degrees of the intensity of being are made immediately accessible to our intuition. By denying the limits of such a specified, immediately accessible intensity of being, by displaying these limits upwards in the direction of pure being, it is possible to determine, in some way, albeit only negatively, extramundane beings as such and not only in their most general determinations, which they share with all beings. We do this as it were in and through their relation to the degrees of being that are immediately known to us. (By such beings we do not mean, of course, only substantial entities, but also states of affairs pertaining to them, and so on.)

The concept of being is not merely a static one, of the most empty and meaningless generality. For all its empty universality it possesses an inner dynamism toward the fullness of being (that is the meaning of the analogy of the concept of being). That is why it has, by itself, the possibility of growing interiorly, as it were, and of taking on a richer content, from within and not through the adding of external properties derived from elsewhere. Thus it becomes possible to let the concept of being, together with its transcendental determinations, grow by and out of itself until, stopped as it were in its dynamism by negation at a certain point, it designates a certain extramundane intensity of being.

Since the onset to this more positive fullness in such a concept always has come from the appearance and remains dependent on it, it remains always necessary to turn [192] toward the appearance in this widening of the concept, by means of negation, up to the level of supramundane being. If we may express this whole state of affairs in a geometrical image, we would say: Suppose a field given in its whole extension, further a certain segment of this whole field, in which certain points may be reached at will and determined immediately, independently of others. In that case it is possible, from these points, to define and determine with certitude every other point of the whole field through its relation to the points immediately accessible and known in themselves.

This does not mean at all, of course, that by ourselves we can, by starting from these our immediately accessible objects, know the actual existence or the inner possibility of each being in the extramundane domain of possibilities. This is excluded already by the simple fact that at least the actual existence of extramundane beings too depends on a free act of God, and that therefore their existence cannot be established by us left to our own devices. The same thing may, at least in some cases, be true of the knowledge of the mere possibility of such facts outside of the world of appearance.

When several negations meet (or eventually necessarily meet) in the concept of such a being, if it is to be conceivable at all for human knowledge, it is quite possible that, on the basis of such a concept alone, the intrinsic possibility of such a being can no longer be known, [193] although this concept does in fact still really reach and define this being and provides a knowledge of it.

To return to our geometrical image: The field of being as such is limitless. This limitlessness is experienced as the absence of a certain limit in the *Vorgriff*, not in its infinity in itself. Hence this field is not for us a clearly defined reality. When, on the basis of two or more points within the field of our experience, we try to define a real or possible point lying outside the intramundane field, it might be impossible to find out whether we are not intending a point that does no longer lie within the field, in other words, something impossible in itself. Nevertheless, if such a doubt is removed by revelation or in some other way, a real knowledge of such a being may be possible by means of such a negative determination.

Thus we have hitherto established what follows: In principle every being may be determined in function of what appears. This determination can take place only through a negation. This does not mean that we can determine every reality in such a way that we can, by ourselves alone, come to know every being in its inner possibility or even in its actual existence. On the other hand, we have already established that an extramundane being cannot, in its own reality, be given to a receptive knowledge. If we take all this together we reach the conclusion that an extramundane being can be given to the finite spirit through the word.

Hence word is no longer here, as it was at an earlier stage of our investigation, meant as merely some kind of vicarious sign, [194] but as a *conceptual* sign of the spirit, immediately intended for the latter. A negation as such can only take place in the word, which is, of course, not the same as a phonetic sound.

Hence every extramundane being may be comprehended in the word. For, on the one hand, the word does not represent the being in itself; on the other hand, through the negation which it (and only it) can assume, it is capable of determining, in function of what appears every being, even one that never appears. Therefore, insofar as it always refers to an appearance, the human word can be the way in which every being may be revealed. Insofar as the human word refers to a concept which, through negation, represents an extramundane being, it may, when spoken by the extramundane God, reveal to humanity the existence and the inner possibility of such a being.

Hence we may summarize our three statements as follows: Even in the appearance alone an extramundane being may be revealed to us by the human word, as the bearer of a concept of such a being derived through negation from the appearance.

We have already seen that we are the beings who must necessarily listen to a possible revelation of the free God. Since we have now shown that everything, including extramundane beings, may be made known by the human word, as it combines negated appearance and negating transcendence, we have also said that we are at least the ones who must listen to a revelation of this free God *in a human word*.

We have shown that the human [195] word does not mean an *a priori* restriction of what may be revealed. The fact that we must wait upon such a word that may eventually be spoken is not limitation of God's freedom to reveal what God pleases. Hence there is no need for inquiring further whether God might also be self-revealing without using such a word that reaches supramundane realities through a negation of the appearance. This would at any rate be possible only by giving up the structure of human knowledge, as we have discovered it, a structure that combines spiritual transcendence and sense appearance. Since we understand ourselves only as endowed with such kind of knowledge, we do not have to wait for a revelation that might take place only if this combination were given up. Whether and why such a revelation might be possible should therefore not further concern us here, especially since it may be shown that such an eventually different kind of revelation must finally be transformed into one whose intrinsic possibility we have just established.

For as long as we are not raised above our basic makeup, as explained above, such a different kind of revelation, should it ever determine and shape our normal being and activity, must be transposed by us into the kind whose structure we have tried to explain, i.e., into one that is comprehended in the human word. This implies that we are the beings who have at least to take into account the occurrence of a revelation of the free God through the human word. But in this way we have already anticipated the more thorough [196] considerations that are still to follow.

Our first task here was to answer the questions how transcendence and historicity are related to each other. What we have called appearance is nothing but what we meet in our history: everything existing within the world, not only the objects that can immediately be known through the senses, but we ourselves too in our whole being and activity, as, through our knowledge of and dealings with the things of the world, we arrive at grasping our own being.

We have now sufficiently answered this question so that we may say: Every transcendent reality may in principle be represented to humanity not only in its most general determinations, but also according to its specific properties. It may be represented negatively through this historical appearance that we call word. This word itself is in its turn the synthesis of an intramundane, historical reality and of a negation. Thus we have established that the word is the place of a possible encounter with and revelation of the free God, before whom, because of our transcendence, we are always already standing.

But this does not yet clearly explain our relation, as historical beings, with a possible revelation. It is true that we have established that we must pay attention to a possible word of God, that is spoken in our human language, and that may nonetheless say everything that is to be revealed. But it has not yet become clear *where* we are to wait for this word. This points to the further question that must occupy us.

[197] We have come to know ourselves as spirit and therefore as those who stand open for the free revelation of God. Thus we have also, because of the peculiar way in which we are spirit, understood that we are historical beings, who, as *spirit,* may come to know *every* being, and as spirits *endowed with senses and living in history,* may come to know every being in the *word,* at least if this word is spoken to us in our human language by the free God. Thus there only remains to find out where we are to hear this word of God as a human word.

In order to find an answer to this question, two of the previously established points must work together: the insight into human historicity, and the insight into the historicity that necessarily belongs to a possible revelation of God.

We start with the historicity which belongs necessarily to God's revelation. We have understood God's revelation as God's free activity with humanity. It remains a possibility, even when our creation by God is already presupposed, because of our finiteness and of our absolute transcendence. Therefore we must always reckon with it. Such a free action of God, which takes place within the empty, but already real space of the human being, is already historical by itself. It is not prehistoric, like the creation of the human being which, although free, had no partner, so that in it God acted only with God alone. Moreover it is not universal and necessary. It is free, hence unforeseeable. We can grasp and understand it only in itself. There is no point, no presupposition in the world, from which [198] its actuality and its proper nature might be determined.

Hence, although we must always reckon with it and wait for it, it is the unexpected. Such a free revelation is, of its very nature, historical, i.e., the unique, gratuitous activity of a free agent. But how does such an activity of God stand in human space? Can it, despite its divine historicity, be humanly *un*historical, i.e., not occupy a certain point in the space and the time of human history? Or is it also essentially historical for us, i.e., shall it, on account of its divine historicity occupy a certain place also in human history, enter in contact with this history and its spatiotemporal extension at a certain point, so that we have to turn toward this specific point of our history if we are to perceive God's revealed word?

We hold that the latter possibility is the one that corresponds to the inner nature of a possible revelation of God. We have already given the reasons above. For we have already said that, in whatever way revelation may originally take place, it has to be transposed into the human word, if it is not to be taken by revelation out of our human way of existing.

It is inadmissible that we should be permanently and miraculously raised above our natural way of thinking and of acting by God's revelation. This would ultimately reduce God's free revelation again to be but an essential element of humanity itself, since we would no longer come to know it as the unexpected, as the act of God's freedom [199] with regard to us as already constituted in our essence. Therefore, at least within the existence of the individual human being, the free revelation can occur only at a definite point. For all other times we can keep revelation only by the way of a human word. We must forever refer back again to this certain exceptional point as to the unique point in human history at which God's revelation has originally emerged. Hence revelation takes place once in human history at least in *this* sense that it cannot be permanently coexistent with all the single moments of a single human history. Thus, in order to meet revelation, humanity must refer back again, in historical knowledge, at least to certain exceptional moments of our own history.

But once we have come that far, there can be no theoretical difficulty in admitting that we must reckon with the possibility that such a revelation does not occur, at a certain point in *every* individual history of each person, but only in the history of *some* individual human beings. As for the whole life of each of us individual persons — who can permanently possess a revelation only by turning back to a certain point of history that can never be repeated, who can possess it only in the words in which it has been expressed — it makes no essential difference whether we have to turn to one point of our *own* history or to one in the history of *another* person, as long as we can come to know at this point of a human history that [200] a revelation has really taken place. There would exist an essential difference only if each of were always able, in our own lives, to repeat this revelation at will in its original form. In that case it would be true that the outer historical demonstration of an original revelation in another person would be no substitute for a revelation experienced from within one's own existence. But this hypothesis stands in contradiction with the free divine historicity of revelation, at least if we presuppose that, in general at least, humankind would continue to exist with our usual human makeup even if a revelation occurs. Hence we must think of the historicity of a possible revelation in itself as historical also in the sense of a *human* history, i.e., we must look out for it as an event that has occurred at a certain point of space and time within the total history of humanity.

The only question which arises then is whether every person is capable of hearing it if it eventually takes place at a point of the total history of mankind that is very remote from oneself. At this stage of our investigation this question is not meant in the sense that we inquire how in fact and concretely the single person may come to the knowledge of such a revelation that happens in history. Rather our question is meant in the sense of a transcendental question, i.e., we inquire merely why on account of our essence we must from the start examine history for an eventual revelation. In other words, we ask why we may not, with regard to human history in general, [201] affect from the start a total indifference and lack of interest, so that the attempt to demonstrate that a revelation has in fact occurred would from the start be totally useless for such a person.

Moreover we now no longer ask this question in the sense of whether we must, because of our essence, take into account a divine revelation. We have already answered this question. The question now is only this: why, because of our essence, must we reckon with a revelation of God that would take place in human history. A demonstration deriving from revelation, from the fact that it must happen in human history, if it happens at all, is not a complete answer to this question, which is not a question about revelation, but about a peculiar property of the one to whom such a revelation is to be addressed.

Chapter 14
The Necessity of Listening for a Revelation Occurring in History. Summary

Revelation is possible. Being is luminous and the human person stands absolutely open for being. It is not true that revelation has always already occurred, for the absolute being is absolute freedom and acts freely with regard to humanity, while we ourselves freely decide about the concrete manner of our openness toward God. The place where such a revelation may occur is our history. The historical appearance in the world may, in the human word, [202] make known the free word of the God of revelation.

So the only remaining question was why we, seen in ourselves, must listen to our own history. The mere fact that revelation, if it comes, comes in history, and that, as a spirit, we ourselves must take a revelation of God into account, is not yet the whole final and explicit answer to this question. For hitherto we have, at least explicitly, considered the historicity of an eventual revelation only from the point of view of the content of such a revelation. We have seen that such a content may be made known in the historical word. Thus we must go on and explicitly ask the question from the standpoint of humankind: Why are we, considered as those who listen for a revelation, to listen for it in our *history?*

We have already prepared the answer to this question. We are historical beings, in and because of our transcendent openness for being as such, which makes us refer to God and thus to a possible revelation. In order to stand before being as such, we must turn toward the appearance. And we have already pointed out that the appearance means not only the single sense object of external experience, but the whole of being in the world, which comprises also the history of humanity, and, insofar as we are always human in humankind, also the history of humankind. Therefore turning toward history is not something optional for us. Because of our specific human spirituality, it is always already basically imposed upon us. [203] Detaching [*Loslösung*] ourselves consciously from our history would put us in intrinsic contradiction with our own nature, not simply insofar as the latter possesses a biological aspect, but with regard to its spiritual aspect. Every time we turn to the appearance, which is essential for all human knowledge, we also turn to something that is always already historical, since the appearance, at least as a fact in human life itself, is a fact that happens just once.

Thus every kind of rationalism, as an attempt to lift human existence above history, must be rejected as inhuman and therefore also as lacking due respect for the human spirit. If we have to be spirit and can be such only by turning toward the appearance, we cannot not be interested in the greatest and fullest possible appearance, in the eventual totality of appearances. For as the appearances increase in variety and number, what the spirit's end is appears more clearly in them: being as such, extending also beyond the world.

Now the appearance which is in itself the most spiritual is humanity itself. Hence we are the appearance which, by itself, can be the fullest appearance for being as such. But what we are appears only in the unfolding reality of possible humanity, in human history as such. That is why, on account of this spiritual nature, we, in order to be spirit, are essentially referred to history. If we stand before the God of a free revelation, if this revelation has to come in human history, if it comes at all (should it not come, [204] the most essential aspect of human history would be God's silence in this history), if we are from the start referred to history, within which this revelation may possibly come, then we are essentially the beings who, in our innermost nature, listens to a possible revelation of God through the word in human history. Only those who listen in this way and only to the extent that they listen in this way, are authentically what they have to be: human.

Thus a metaphysical anthropology turns into an ontology of the obediential potency for a possible free revelation. The philosophy of religion is the analytic study of humanity as we must listen for a possible revelation. And every natural religion, that might be constructed with the help of such an anthropology and metaphysics has understood its own nature only when it is itself the listening to and reckoning with a possible revelation of God in human history.

We feel that, in this way, we have in the main answered the question which we asked at the start of our considerations. Thus there only remain two things to do: to summarize once more, so as to get an overview of the road we have travelled; and to put our answer explicitly in connection with the problems with which, at the start, we had confronted our topic.

The question with which we started our considerations about the philosophy of religion was the following: What relation exists between philosophy of religion and theology? We claimed that this was an epistemological question, which might, in final analysis, be answered only if we inquired into the one ground from [205] which both these sciences emerge in their diversity and in their mutual relation. Thus our question became one about the nature of the human person as about ourselves as the beings who, owing to the fact that, in our metaphysics, we develop a philosophy of religion, become listeners for a possible revelation. That is why the philosophy of religion was not for us the construction of a natural religion, based upon itself and complete within itself; it consisted in showing us to be the finite spirits who, because of our nature, are turned toward a possible revelation of God. A philosophy of religion, which understands itself in this way, is a part of general metaphysics. It is ultimately general metaphysics itself, since every metaphysical question contains the whole of metaphysics within itself.

Thus we had to engage in metaphysics. A science that inquires about being as such can possess no previous knowledge that it holds for certain, that it takes for granted, from which it simply starts. Hence the starting point of metaphysics must be the general question about being itself, taken however with the necessity it always possesses in human existence. This question about being had three aspects. Thus we had to examine in three different sections what this unavoidable question can tell us about the nature of being. Since the general question about being is the starting point insofar as we necessarily bring it up, it always also contains a statement about the very being of us who bring it up. What is being as such and in general? That was the question. The procedure and the conclusion of our analysis may be summarized as follows:

[206] 1) We inquire about being as such. It follows:

a) For the nature of being as such: Being is self-presence. A being as such, and to the extent that it possesses being, is luminous and knowable. For our philosophy of religion this yields the insight that every reality whatsoever, considered in itself, may be a possible object of a revelation in this sense that no being is, by itself, unable to become manifest to knowledge. Being as such is, in the most general sense, utterable.

b) For human nature: To be human is to be spirit. We are transcendence toward being as such. In every judgment, i.e., every time a self-subsisting being knows an object, hence in every activity, we reach for [*Vorgriff*] being as such. Thus we are human because we are transcendence toward being as such. Our openness is not a relative one; it does not extend merely to a certain sector of the real or of the possible. It is absolutely unlimited. For a philosophy of religion this means: As spirit we are, by our innermost being, always already referring to the absolute being of God. We head for God, and in such a way that, because of its unlimited range, our transcendence constitutes no restricting *a priori* law for what might possibly be revealed.

Thus we may summarize the two conclusions of our first section in this statement: Being as such has for us as spirits an ultimate fundamental luminosity.

[207] 2) We must inquire about being as a whole. We not only affirm the luminosity of being, we must also *inquire* about being. This entails that we who inquire are not pure being, self-luminous and without questions. We grasp ourselves as finite. Thus the necessity of the question about being, which includes the necessary affirmation of the being of the inquirers themselves, contains a voluntary affirmation of contingent and fortuitous finite being. Hence it follows:

a) For God, the pure absolute being: With regard to every finite being pure being stands in its total luminosity as the supremely *free* being. For our philosophy of religion this means that the God before whom we stand in our transcendence, is the free one.

The possibilities of God's freedom are not exhausted by the free creation of the finite spirit. Hence, in divine freedom, God stands before us as what is the most deeply hidden, as self-revelation to us in the openness of our transcendence only when and insofar as God freely wills. Thus we always and essentially stand before a God of a possible revelation who may freely display or freely hide divine possibilities.

b) For humankind: Within human transcendence toward the pure being of God there occurs a voluntary attitude. Insofar as our free voluntary attitude toward to the values, finite or grasped as finite, reacts upon the horizon under which we know and will our values, it may be seen that the concrete form of our transcendence is always also the act of our free decision. [208] For our philosophy of religion this means that as finite spirits our openness for the free God of a possible revelation is not as such a purely theoretical concern of a neutral spirituality, but it is, as such, a free decision, *religio*. In itself it is already our free yielding to this God of a possible revelation.

Thus we may summarize the two conclusions of the second section in the one statement: The human person as a finite spirit stands in free decision before the free God of a possible revelation.

3) We must inquire about being while keeping in mind the distinction between being and beings. This follows from the fact that our spirituality is a receptive one. The receptivity of human knowledge implies possessing a sensibility, as a power that emanates from the spirit and thus implies our being [*forma*] in matter. Thus we see that we are historical beings in the sense that, although we are capable of knowing being as a whole, we can do so only by turning toward a historical appearance in the world. It follows:

a) For a possible revelation of God considered in itself: Such a revelation is possible, and it occurs, if it occurs, in the human word that, as unity of appearance and of transcendental openness of the spirit toward being as such may, through negation, be a sign for absolutely everything, even the extramundane being. And this human word that reveals God is itself a historical event within the general history of mankind.

[209] b) For us: Insofar as we are spirit and must therefore reckon with a possible revelation of the free God, and insofar as

we can be spirit only as historical beings, we must turn toward the history of humanity, so as to meet in it God's possible revelation.

Thus we may summarize the two conclusions of the third section in one sentence: Humankind must in our human history listen for the historical revelation of God which may come in the human word.

We may therefore summarize our whole anthropology by saying as it were by way of a definition: We are the beings of receptive spirituality, who stand in freedom before the free God of a possible revelation, which, if it comes, happens in our history through the word. We are the ones who, in our history, listen for the word of the free God. Only thus are we what we should be. A metaphysical anthropology has reached its end when it has understood itself as the metaphysics of an obediential potency for the revelation of the supramundane God.

Of course, in this way, we have by no means even touched upon all the questions which might come up for such an ontology of the obediential potency for a possible revelation. By way of appendix we may draw attention at least to a few points.

Thus we would still have to answer the question how a human word spoken in history may be recognized as that of the supramundane God. In the line of our previous approach we would first have to answer: Since the human word is supposed to refer to an extramundane being [210] through the fact that, by means of negation, an appearance points toward this extramundane reality, we must show that this negation is objectively valid and does not rest upon an arbitrary human decision.

This would help us develop a metaphysical concept of the miracle, which does not, from the start, stress its physical side as an exception to a law of nature. Its own original starting point should emphasize the miracle's character as a "sign" of the God of revelation. The exception made to the innerwordly natural connections must be considered from the start as a sign addressed to us, as we listen already to revelation. By "negating" these natural connections this sign testifies to the objectivity of the negation occurring in the revealed word.

Another question must concern the concrete way in which the historical experience of an individual person can penetrate to the historical event of a revelation, especially when, in outside time, this revelation is quite distant from this individual. We would have to analyze more precisely the historical determination of the individual spiritual life. This would lead us into the problem of the temporality of the spiritual history of humanity, a temporality that does not merely consist in applying astronomical time to the physical process of human history. It represents a more original and peculiar category previous to and independent of physical time. In this way the historical ties of a certain person with an event that (measured in physical time) belongs to the past, might turn out to be as human history, a simultaneity. [211] We would find out that events of a human history as such do not occur in the same sense as and with the same rhythm as physical occurrences. We would have to examine the metaphysical concept of tradition that is of fundamental importance for our spiritual nature. In the original sense, we turn to "past" history not through "historical studies." We do so when, in a living tradition (measured in the time of human history) this "past" remains present, and is not properly speaking always still in the making. Once these and other concepts of human historicity have been elaborated, they might be applied to the history of revelation, taking of course into consideration the changes they undergo by entering into the history of God's relation with humanity. But for the time being these vague hints will have to do.

Thus there only remains the task of explicitly understanding the conclusions we have reached as answer to the most general question about the relation between philosophy of religion and theology. In accordance with the two first chapters this task will have to be carried out in the following way: First we must answer this question immediately exactly as it sounds. This corresponds to the content of the first chapter. Secondly this answer will be illustrated by the threefold relation our question has with the related problems mentioned in the second chapter.

V. Conclusion

Chapter 15
The Philosophy of Religion and Theology

It is now our task to put the conclusion of our investigation explicitly within the context in which we have envisioned our question in the first two chapters.

In the first chapter we had first been concerned immediately with the relation between philosophy of religion and theology. We started there from an epistemological standpoint. We had to determine the mutual relation of two sciences. Such a relation does not come about after these sciences have been fully developed. We must rather consider them originally, as they come into their own, as sciences which are from the start different yet related.

From the start we have seen that theology in the Catholic sense of the word, as a listening to the personal revelation of the supremely free and transcendent God to humanity, cannot be set up in function of humanity, that it always rests on the fact of such a Logos of God. All sciences are, in a true sense, anthropology, except for theo-logy. All of them, irrespective [213] of their reference to things, are based in their reality and procedures upon the logos of humanity; they are the "things in the spirit of humankind."

Theology alone exists because there is a word of God to humanity. It is true that, when we consider theology as a whole, we may distinguish in it a double moment: the simple listening to God's message and the systematic elaboration of what has been heard under formal points of view, that belong to human spirituality itself. The second aspect, which we may traditionally call Scholastic, speculative theology (as opposed to positive theology), is in itself at first a human undertaking. God's perceived message becomes in it, as it were, the "topic" on which we reflect according to the formal principles with which in other domains too, we try to assimilate intellectually some topic that occurs to us. Of course, an epistemology of a theology understood in this way would have to answer many more questions: the possibility and the meaning of such an intellectual, systematic elaboration of the divine message, the limits of such an enterprise, its method, its relation to theology in the first sense, and so on.

However, when speaking of theology in this work we meant it always in the first sense, of the kerygma itself, of the simple listening to God's word itself, of the acceptance in faith of the message itself, not of the metaphysical elaboration of what was heard or believed. And of such a theology it is true that it exists because God speaks, not because we think; what appears in this theology is God, not, as in all other sciences, humanity in its essence.

Yet even in such a science humanity cannot [214] simply be overlooked or eliminated, since there would exist no word of God, if there were not someone who would at least be capable of perceiving it. Hence there exists a theological anthropology. Not simply in the proper and strict sense, that God, in the divine Logos, manifests to us the ultimate structure of our own human nature, so that a theological anthropology is part of the *content* of theology. But there exists also a "theological" anthropology in the sense that some, albeit naive, unreflective self-understanding of human beings is the condition of the possibility of theology. For not only must the listening to a coming revelation presuppose a certain basic human makeup but also, as a listening in freedom, know and accept it. The word of God itself must, if it is to be perceived, be able to resound like a human word, and this again presupposes a certain makeup human nature itself.

It follows that theology presupposes a "theological" anthropology which may be called fundamental theological anthropology. What we have elaborated in all these lectures was nothing but this fundamental theological anthropology which, of course, like every metaphysical science, comprises and sets in motion the whole of metaphysics. Thus we arrive finally at the question: 1) what relation does this fundamental theological anthropology have to the philosophy of religion, as generally understood? And 2) if both these sciences are identical, at least in their core, what is the relation between theology and this philosophy of religion which turns out to be a fundamental theological anthropology?

[215] 1) We may answer the first question as follows: Such a fundamental theological anthropology, as we have tried to present in its main outline, is the authentic philosophy of religion. What we have been doing is anthropology insofar as we treated of humanity; it is theological anthropology, insofar as we understood ourselves as the beings who, in freedom, have to listen to the possible message of the free God. It is a fundamental theological anthropology insofar as this self-understanding which we have of ourselves is presupposed by our capability of hearing the theology that actually exists. This fundamental theological anthropology is the real philosophy of religion. We must still show this in more detail.

We start from the usual idea of philosophy of religion which, in the formal neutrality of its definition, does not seem to say anything yet about this at first surprising thesis that for us as believers and as philosophers, the philosophy of religion, in its true and complete concept and content, can be nothing but precisely the above mentioned fundamental theological anthropology.

First, if we consider the word itself, the philosophy of religion is the philosophical determination of what religion is and has to be. Thus philosophy of religion is first of all philosophy, i.e., it uses the tools of knowledge that belong properly to philosophy in general. Hence it determines religion from a standpoint which is from the start and always at its disposal: from the indestructible nature of humanity, from the world that goes necessarily together with human being, from the evident and necessary formal principles of thinking, in fine, [216] from what is usually called the natural light of reason.

It is in this way that we try to determine the nature of religion. We have here neither the opportunity nor the intention of enumerating the different conclusions that have been reached in the course of history in such attempts. It is enough simply to observe that a philosophy of religion that does not intend to be a mere description of the cultural phenomenon of religion, but that inquires about the truth and the nature of authentic religion as a whole, must at any rate come to the knowledge of the transcendent, absolute and personal God. Thus it acknowledges religion as the existential bond between humanity as a whole and this

God. All empirical observable "religions" are religions only insofar as they succeed in thus connecting us existentially to the
real, living God.

From this formal determination of the philosophy of religion and of religion, it follows first that such a philosophy of
religion comprises a metaphysical anthropology. Of course not
in the sense that there is no formal distinction between a metaphysical anthropology and a philosophy of religion, and that both
would simply be one and the same thing. But in such a way that
in its statements either science already comprises essentially and
necessarily the other one. This is true for two simple reasons.
First, the philosophical knowledge of God (the heart of a nor-
mative philosophy of religion) is possible only within the one
science of metaphysics. Natural theology is not a philosophical
science based upon itself, which would share with other philosophical disciplines [217] only the basic principles of formal logic.
It is but an inner moment of the general doctrine of being, of
metaphysics.

Every philosophy knows about God only insofar as and because it knows of being as such, and this simply for the reason
that absolute being in itself is not immediately accessible to it.
Now if natural theology is conceivable only as a moment of general ontology, then whatever belongs essentially to the latter, is
also part of the former. But a general ontology is always also
already a metaphysical anthropology. For in general ontology
we speak of being in general not merely in the sense of the empty
logical uniformity of "something" (this concept would never do
for an adequate determination of the absolute being, as required
by a philosophy of religion). It is taken rather in the sense of an
analogical ontological concept of being. This concept may be
predicated of all beings, but in such a way that in it we are always already aware of what being properly is in its increasing
purity and fullness. That is why we know that this concept can
only be used analogically.

But this is possible only if as philosophers we immediately
reach at least in one spot a being that is itself in some sense this
transcendent fullness of being. This being is the spirit. The spirit
can do ontology only if it has grasped itself as spirit. For only
then can it know what being is properly, analogically. Only then

can we know that in its purity and fullness, being is properly spirit. Only then can we construct at least an analogical concept of God, which may make possible a religion. This implies that a general ontology, and hence a natural theology, [218] are always already intrinsically carried by an anthropology, by our knowledge of ourselves.

The philosophy of religion is a natural theology and the latter is possible only in a unity with a metaphysical anthropology. In this unity and interaction, we come to know the nature of being by knowing the spirit, and to know the nature of the spirit as a modification of being as such, so that every deepening of the concept of being helps us better to know human being and the other way round.

The connection between philosophy of religion and metaphysical anthropology appears even more simply and more clearly from the following consideration: the philosophy of religion, as it establishes our existential bond with God, not only has to know about God, but also us, who have to have this bond with God. Thus every philosophy of religion is also necessarily a statement about our nature; it implies a metaphysical anthropology.

Thus we have shown that, even if we adopt a formal and seemingly neutral conception of the philosophy of religion, the latter turns out to be a metaphysical anthropology.

When we keep in mind what was said above, it is easy to see that, as an inner moment of the philosophy of religion, such an anthropology turns necessarily into a fundamental theological anthropology in the sense explained above. For this metaphysical anthropology, as we worked it out, in a purely philosophical way, showed us to be the beings who stand necessarily in freedom before the God of a possible revelation. Such a metaphysical anthropology is a fundamental theology.

Whatever [219] other characteristics an anthropology may discover in us, it will be unable to ignore the ones we have mentioned. And when such a philosophy of religion, basing itself upon such an anthropology, sets out to say how the religion of such a humanity must be before such a God, it will have to require that humanity should stand ready to perceive in history the living word of the free God.

In a word, whatever the philosophy of religion may be or must be when we consider it in itself alone, it will always be a fundamental theological anthropology whose last word is the summons to listen for God's word. And since such a word has in fact been spoken, a philosophy of religion has nothing more to do than to outline such a fundamental theological anthropology. For whatever else it may, with the natural light of reason, discover about human religion, has been superseded in fact by revealed religion. Thus such considerations of the philosophy of religion no longer have the same existential significance they would have if God had not spoken and if we had only to listen to silence. If by philosophy and metaphysics we do not mean in the first place thinking for thinking's sake, but an activity prompted by our existential needs, we must say that a philosophy of religion that is possible in itself, but whose content has lost all existential impact, is no longer philosophy and metaphysics in the same sense as that part of it which is constituted by fundamental theological anthropology.

[220] 2) This allows us now to determine explicitly and to define the relation between the philosophy of religion and theology. When the philosophy of religion is what it ought to be, it is fundamental theological anthropology. This explains its specific character with regard to theology. It is philosophy and only philosophy. But it is human philosophy and human metaphysics, an effort of the human spirit to grasp being.

That is why its originally innermost, first and last attitude is and remains: the ready openness and the open readiness for theology. It cannot force theology, or deduce it, or impose laws upon it. But it constitutes a being that can listen, should God's Logos come into this world. And since God has come and must always be listened to, its task is enduring and lasting; it is the task of *"facienti quod in se est Deus non denegat gratiam"* ["God does not refuse grace to those who do their best"] in the domain of knowledge; it is already a moral decision, as much as any we generally designate by this name, so that this theological axiom rightly applies to it. Thus philosophy of religion is not the same as theology on another level, or with other means, or something that merely constructs a hypothetical order that would prevail if there were no theology. It is that which prepares for theology; as such it is the latter's necessary presupposition. With the thoroughness of scientific research it establishes the obediential potency for revelation.

We must next inquire why the philosophy of religion as fundamental theological anthropology lets theology be exclusively based [221] on the word of God. An explicit answer to this question no longer needs lengthy considerations. The philosophy of religion, as human knowledge of being unlimited spirit standing before the free God of a possible revelation, cannot decide in advance what may be the possible content of such a speaking of God, cannot even say whether God will ever speak. The fact that there exists someone who listens for the word or the silence of God in no way affects the reality or the manner of the religion deriving from God's spoken revelation. Since the listening, considered from our point of view, must as well reckon with a silence of God, God's self-manifestation remains in every respect an unforeseeable and undue grace.

Although listening to God is the condition of hearing God's word and although this listening is our free activity in our correct existential self-understanding, theology remains based upon itself. First, because listening does not necessarily imply any actual hearing (neither in fact nor for the content). Perceiving God's silence is also an answer that makes the listening meaningful. Under God's silence too we may become what we have to be at any rate: personal finite spirit before the personal infinite free God, with whom we necessarily have to deal, at least by being aware of God's silence.

And second, because the mystery by which the freely self-constituting listener, in a concrete free act, despite all its autonomy, stands under the influx of God's free grace, even that factual realization of the condition which makes possible a listening [222] to theology was still a free action of God before it became our free action. And since God brings about the readiness for listening *as* a condition for hearing God's own word, theology is wholly based upon itself: the word of the living God. The philosophy of religion is previous to it only as a condition. And even as such it comes from the self-revealing God. Hence it is a condition of receptive theology only insofar as it is conditioned by God's word.

Thus we have explained the relation existing between the philosophy of religion and theology, insofar as this is possible from the standpoint of the philosophy of religion (we have already mentioned at the start that not all problems are covered in this way). We may shed some more light upon these conclusions by briefly referring to the questions by means of which we had explained our problem in the second chapter. We had then brought up three questions in relation with our topic: the usual procedure of fundamental theology; the problem of the possibility of a Christian philosophy; the solutions suggested by Protestant philosophy of religion.

1) In the usual procedure of fundamental theology we regretted the absence of a more explicit discussion of the problem of the relation existing between metaphysical knowledge and the knowledge derived from divine revelation. To put it more exactly, the problem was how we human beings could be the recipients for such revealed knowledge without being entitled to demand it as the necessary end of our immanent development, as something "due" to us. Or again, how we could be understood as the ones who possibly hear an unexpected word of God, how we are obliged to [223] listen for it in our history.

We may have at least discovered the outline of an answer to these questions of fundamental theology. We are spirit, hence absolute openness "upwards," i.e., for all being. Thus we are also the recipients of a possible revelation. But precisely because, through our mere transcendence, we are spirit, real infinity is never presented to us as actually reached, but always only as the ever greater beyond of our knowing, only as anticipation [*Vorgriff*]. Thus we stand as finite spirit before the personal, free, and absolute God.

We possess our transcendence always only as that which surpasses every available knowledge. This is so true that, from our point of view, it is impossible to understand how the anticipation and the actually possessed and fulfilled knowledge can ever perfectly cover each other. We stand before God as before the one who is and forever remains free. It follows that, precisely because we are the openness for being as such, we face the real possibility of a revelation, at least insofar as it is the free personal self-manifestation of a divine *Thou*. Such a revelation can never be superseded by an autonomous human claim on knowledge. We have also already explained that and why such a revelation is historical, and must be expected in human history. Thus our fundamental theological anthropology would in fact be the part we usually do not find, or do not find explicitly enough in the usual fundamental theology: the analysis of the obediential potency for revelation.

2) This shows also to what extent philosophy as such is and can be Christian in an original sense. Not in the first place [224] because theology is a protective negative norm for philosophy or obliges it to consider theological problems metaphysically. We would then have to call it Scholastic theology rather than philosophy. Philosophy as real philosophy is Christian because, as fundamental theological anthropology, it "sublates" itself into theology. And insofar as it makes of us those who listen to a possible revelation to God, it always and in every case sublates itself into "theology." For even should God keep silent, the person who does such metaphysics perceives a word of God: silence. And even in this case the last existentially decisive human attitude would be a humble submission to this silent God and the human person would in a certain sense be a "theologian."

It is always constitutive and essential for human philosophy to be ready to give up its existential character as a clarification of existence in behalf of a theo-logy and to "sublate" itself in the above mentioned sense. Correctly understood, philosophy is always an expectation, a preparation for the Gospel. In this sense it is Christian by itself, not in the sense of some subsequent baptism, but by the fact that it sets up someone who can hear God's message, insofar as such a power of hearing derives from human nature.

3) Finally we may also understand why and how a philosophy of religion, that is really Christian in this sense, is the authentic fundamental unity and synthesis of the two basic Protestant types of philosophy of religion.

On the one hand, our philosophy of religion as fundamental theological anthropology [225] establishes a positive human receptivity for revelation, so that this receptivity is not simply the negative dialectical repercussion, not merely the critical judgment pronounced on all that is human and innerworldly. On the other hand, this receptivity turns out not to be such that, with respect to it, revelation would not simply be another word for an immanently demanded fulfillment of this religious receptivity and God only its necessary immanent correlate. Thus God can really still speak, and, on the other hand, we can hear this word of God, which we cannot deduce by ourselves, in such a way that we really perceive it.

Our considerations have shown that a correctly conceived "intellectualism" (i.e., one that considers human persons as free historical spirits, who must enact [*vollziehen*] in a "world" the spiritualization that leads us up to the absolute spirit) does not run as much danger of transforming revelation into an intrahuman event, belonging to human nature, as a philosophy of religion that makes of feeling, experience, and other such phenomena the proper place of religion.

If we are historical spirits before the free God, we stand open also for a positive fulfillment of our obediential potency which, as spirit, we necessarily possess. Revelation does not have to be merely a critical judgment pronounced on what is human, merely something standing above the world, which can never become "flesh" but always only a thorn in the flesh. Yet, on the other hand, we can and must accept God's free revelation as unexpected, undue grace, as "history," not as opposed to nature but as standing above nature.

Thus we have arrived at the end of our considerations. [226] It might seem that we had not achieved much. But let us suppose for one moment at least that we should really have succeeded in bringing to a good end what we intended to do. We should then, on the theoretical level, have put into concepts what we must do in our existential decisions, when we have to look for an answer to the question whether the living God does not wish to come to encounter us in human history and in our own personal lives. If and insofar as we have succeeded therein, we have undertaken something important.

Let us suppose ourselves to be convinced that it belongs to the essential and basic attitudes of a life that we have to inquire and to search whether the living God has not, in a wholly determined here and now of human history uttered the decisive word of our personal self-manifestation and that this word is for us in the most proper sense existential, i.e., decisive and disposing of our whole destiny. Let us further suppose that we are convinced that such a word of God, which is to be the existential ground of our lives has, of its very nature, to emerge in human historicity, hidden, as far as its appearance is concerned, as a human word, hence exposed to all that is fortuitous and irritating in history for the eyes of reason with its eternal ideas that remain always clear and lucid.

Then we might wonder whether to be convinced of the above statements is not already to have behind us the greatest part of the way to the Christian faith of the Catholic Church, insofar as the intellectual aspect of living decision is concerned. [227] Let us imagine knowing from the start that we may and must reckon with a historical religion, one that can be reached only by accepting and turning to a historical here and now, that cannot be analyzed in intellectual statements, that is not simply the correlate of a religious feeling or experience or any other religious disposition. Because it reaches us precisely *as* revelation of God in human historicity, it carries with it all that in historical phenomena is fortuitous and unclear, that might have been different and is likely to be criticized. Now, when somebody is ready, from the start, to consider the possibility of such a religion, is it hard for such a person to acknowledge the Holy Roman Catholic Church as the place of the real revelation of the living God?

As far as concerns the claim of the Church with regard to all non-Christian religions, all attempts of the modern history of religions, which try to bring Christianity down to one of the many stages and forms of humanity's religious attitude do not start from an *a posteriori* observation of the factual likeness between Christianity and other religions. This whole research stands already from the start under the more or less explicitly stated *a priori* that there can be no revelation of the living God at a privileged spot of human history, with exclusion of the others. For them it can only be a question of the how (not of the fact) of a history of all religions, in which all of them have to be reduced to the same denominator, because a "supernatural" history of one religion, in contrast to all others, is excluded from the start.

[228] The parallels that can really be established *a posteriori* between Christianity and non-Christian religions may also be

explained in fact without accepting this false *a priori* principle of
the modern history of religion. They may be explained by the
simple fact that here and there we are concerned obviously with
the same human person and that our expectation and looking
out for a real revelation of God, when not fulfilled or not considered as fulfilled, easily evokes similar substitute formations.

However, those who do not share this *a posteriori* prejudice
and who have not, from the start, given up the courage of the
absolute within the finite, cannot find it difficult to establish the
essentially qualitative difference of Christianity from all other
religions, to recognize the Church as the sign raised among the
nations [*signum elevatum in nationibus*], as she testifies by herself
that she is the place of God's revelation, always, of course, in the
presupposition that one takes into account a possible historical
revelation of God. This is presupposed, if one is to be able to see
Christianity in its qualitative difference. Otherwise one comes
up with *a priori* arbitrary demands for the historical form of Christianity, demands which Christianity, as God's history, coming
under the guise of *human* history, can, of course, never satisfy.

As for what concerns the church in relation to the other forms
of Christianity (we are thinking especially of Protestantism —
the situation is somewhat different with the Orthodox Church)
we might say that since they themselves no longer have the [229]
courage (which they should have) to consider themselves exclusively as the place of God's revelation as such, and this in their
own historical uniqueness, we are entitled not to mention them.

We may speak of a historical revelation of God only when
its historical appearance makes as such the claim of "outside the
Church no salvation" [*extra ecclesiam nulla salus*], the claim to be,
as visible and historical event and with exclusion of all others,
the place at which alone the free God of a revelation can be adequately reached, where religion as a really successful bond between the whole person and God (something which cannot be
established from our standpoint alone) has become a reality.

When this courage is lacking, when one claims at the most
only a certain preference above other forms of Christian religion, one gives up the historical uniqueness of God's word and
together with it the courage of believing in a real revelation of
God. In fine, whoever considers the possibility that a certain

sector of human history might be, with exclusion of all others, history of God, can really be and become nothing else than Catholic. We have discovered that the essential core of the philosophy of religion and its essential relation to theology consisted precisely in considering such a possibility.

CPSIA information can be obtained at www.ICGtesting.com
Printed in the USA
LVOW12s2139060813

346673LV00006B/177/A